What people are saying about *Open to Outcome, 2ⁿᵈ Edition*...

"*Open to Outcome, 2ⁿᵈ Edition* is a remarkably concise volume, in which Micah and Mari have put together a near-perfect mix of theory, science, training, tips, and advice for new (and old) facilitators, leaders, and teachers/coaches. I know that in this tiny book, my staff/students are getting a huge resource that will make them better facilitators."—**Ben Oliver, Assistant Director, Colgate University Outdoor Education, Hamilton, NY**

"*Open to Outcome, 2ⁿᵈ Edition* and The 5 Questions is the most universally applicable facilitation tool I know. It changed the way I run my classroom teaching and my leadership training. I purchase copies for new teachers and administrators every year." —**Krista Gypton, 2008 Arizona Ambassador for Excellence**

"This short, powerful book changed the way I think about the way I think. I use The 5 Question model everyday with staff and students to generate genuine, reflective conversations. It's brilliant." —**John Alongi, Assistant Principal, Vacaville High School, CA**

"Jacobson and Ruddy have outlined a framework for anyone to connect experience to learning. The 5 Questions allow a novice to build confidence and the expert to ensure precision. In *Open to Outcome, 2ⁿᵈ Edition*, I realized the knowledge I held so valuable as a manager and facilitator and realized I can impact my current role. This book provides clarity and simplicity to the process of cooperative learning, active engagement, and reflective practice."
—**Nicholas Hagemann, Former NAU Challenge Course Manager, Current 5ᵗʰ Grade Teacher, Portland, OR**

"Reading *Open to Outcome, 2 Edition* is like spending an afternoon in conversation with Micah and Mari. It is an easy to read, comprehensive guide to creating opportunities for transformative learning with groups of all kinds. The 5 Questions provide the reader with a veritable toolbox of techniques that foster a genuine sense of curiosity and mutual understanding between facilitator and participant. It's a go-to references in my practice as an educator."
—Nancy Zigrovic, Teacher, Modern Languages, Iroquois Ridge High School, Oakville, Ontario, Canada

"I highly recommend *Open to Outcome, 2nd Edition* for anyone who works with people. This book provides a framework of strategies that helps move conversations in a positive direction. The messages behind 'open to outcome' are positively instilled in daily interactions with students, teachers, parents, and community members." **—Tom Dreiling, Principal, North Olmsted Middle School, North Olmsted, Ohio**

"I credit the approach taken with The 5 Questions in *Open to Outcome, 2nd Edition* as a major influence in the success of our freshman orientation program—Maroon Round Up! Our junior and senior mentors have embraced the concept of activity and reflection. Students, teachers, and facilitators use the questions to help each other think about how their present actions can be reflected upon to guide future learning and transition into high school." **—Nicole Griffith, Director, Academy for Global Studies, Austin High School, Austin, Texas**

Open to Outcome

**A Practical Guide for Facilitating
& Teaching Experiential Reflection**

Open to Outcome

A Practical Guide for Facilitating & Teaching Experiential Reflection

MICAH JACOBSON
MARI RUDDY

Published by:

Wood N Barnes Publishing & Distribution
2309 N. Willow, Suite A, Bethany, OK 73008
(405) 942-6812

2nd Edition © 2015, Micah Jacobson, Mari Ruddy, and Wood N
Barnes Publishing & Distribution, U.S.A. All rights reserved.

International copyright protection is reserved under Universal
Copyright Convention and bilateral copyright relations of the
U.S.A.

No part of this book may be reproduced, stored in a retrieval
system, or transmitted in any form or by any means, electronic,
mechanical, photocopying, recording or otherwise, without ex-
press written permission of the author and publisher.

Cover Design by Blue Design
Photography by Blue Design
Interior Design by Ramona Cunningham

Printed in the United States of America
ISBN # 978-1-939019-16-5

Contents

*I'd like to dedicate this 2nd edition of
Open to Outcome to my incredible
grandmother, Leah Jacobson.
Born in 1917, my Bubbe Leah has led a life of
kindness, joy, and continuous learning.
She is the shining example in our family of
compassion, sensitivity, wit, and understanding.
We love you very much!
M. J.*

Foreword

I was first exposed to The 5 Questions in my seventh year as a classroom teacher. Recently married with a toddler at home, I was feeling overwhelmed and disillusioned with my career choice. Attending Micah's workshop on being "open to outcome" was a turning point. I learned the five questions, and thought, "Sure, I'll try this. Can't hurt." I bought the book and read it on my trip home. Like a hero in a classic story or myth, I had no idea how powerful my new knowledge was until I returned to the classroom.

Before learning The 5 Questions, I was teaching the same ways I was taught, sage on the stage, direct instruction, and lecture. Too many of my kids were failing, and disruptive behavior was an annoying, persistent problem. So, fresh from the conference, I entered my familiar classroom ready to see if these questions really worked. It didn't take long for one of my students to create a perfect opportunity to field test the model. I resisted the rote response I could feel building up, "How many times have I said ...," and instead I took a deep breath and tried the first question.

"Did you notice you were flicking Alex in the ear instead of working on your essay?"

The student looked at me like I was speaking Aramaic. "Ummm, yeah."

"Why were you choosing to bother Alex instead of writing?"

"I don't have my brainstorming from yesterday."

I couldn't believe it. The questions were working. Instead of bickering with me, or making excuses, we were talking.

"Does this happen in life and school, does this forgetting of things happen often?" I asked.

"Yeah, I'm always forgetting stuff. Some nights I'm at my dad's house, others at my mom's, and I can't always keep it straight. I pretty much forget everything." The boy was making eye contact with me, leaning in. I could see the connection we were building in his body language. "I kinda hate it, I can't keep track of my stuff because I'm always getting moved back and forth."

At first, I was shocked that we had suddenly stumbled onto the root of not just today's difficulty, but the cause of a lot of his issues that year. "What could you do to avoid forgetting things, if you know you will be moving a lot? Who could help you? Where could you put your bag to ensure it doesn't get lost in the shuffle?"

"My backpack. I need to keep track of it, maybe even put all my stuff in it and keep it with me?"

"So, what will you do now?" I asked, a bit unnerved that something I learned at a conference actually worked and in awe of the depth and importance of the information we had just uncovered.

He looked at me, and I swear, I actually saw the light bulb go on. "If I make sure I always keep my backpack with me, no matter what, I'll be okay. I could keep my phone charger, and my Game Boy®, and my inhaler in it!" He was talking faster, excited at this new idea of his.

"Okay, now, head to your seat, get some key ideas down from what you remember from your brainstorming. Tomorrow I will see you with your brainstorming, and your hands to yourself, and your backpack."

He smiled and literally skipped back to his seat. From then on, he made a big deal out of having his backpack with him when he walked into class. It was our little inside thing. I certainly talked to him many more times about making good choices, keeping his hands to himself, staying seated, and, well, normal stuff for a teacher and a young learner. The big change was I didn't yell, and he didn't lower his eyes and nod blankly. We talked, each time uncovering a new truth. At the end of the semester, his grade had gone up by 30%. Years later when he graduated, he gave me a hug and said, "Thanks for taking the time to care when I was an annoying little freshman who couldn't remember my backpack."

From that time on, almost every student conversation with "Did you notice ..."? Then I simply listened and asked and together we uncovered their truths. I no longer had discipline problems in my classroom. I haven't raised my voice in frustration or anger since I first read *Open to Outcome*. In the first two weeks of school, students do what they normally do, I do what I do, we have conversations that begin, "Did you notice ...?" and we go from there. On almost every occasion we find a place of common understanding and an action plan, and we can get back to the business of learning, which is the whole point of being a teacher.

We will always have kids who choose not to follow rules, who are distracted, hurt, sad, hungry, and/or bored. We will always have kids who are advanced, unchallenged, and restless. We will always have kids who are cruising through our halls with a solid B average and little desire to shake anything up. Challenging behavior will always be there, in and out of school. And that is fine, great even, because The 5 Questions are there and they work. They bring people together around a shared experience and create a plan, an action item, and because its creation is shared, it builds community and connection as it plays out.

I could fill books with examples of kids, teachers, fellow parents, and educators who have benefited from the simple yet powerful 5 Question model. It is my go-to mind-set and tool in processing with any and all people, and though my wife is occasionally frustrated when I start a conversation with "Did you notice...?," I know the *Open to Outcome, 2nd Edition* model has made me a better teacher, coach, spouse, and father. For that I am eternally grateful and thankful.

Kevin Ozar
Instructional Coach/Classroom Teacher
Farmington Public Schools, Michigan
July 26, 2015

2nd Edition Introduction

. . . .

It's been more than 11 years since we first published *Open to Outcome*. Since that time, The 5 Questions have been taught to tens of thousands of educators and students. We have been incredibly pleased to see so many new and old facilitators improving their skills in processing experiences.

This second edition is important for several reasons. First and foremost, we have learned and adapted the model over the last 11 years. By carefully watching student implementation, getting feedback from teachers and facilitators and in noticing our own experience with the model, we have observed and integrated improvements to the model and increased our knowledge of successful use of The 5 Questions.

In particular, this edition has two changes to the 5 questions themselves. The 4th question is now an "anchor stage" question with any of the "five Ws" appropriate to help anchor the generalization: Who? What? Where? When? Why? This allows facilitators and teachers a little more flexibility and makes the model more useful given the often-random responses of students. The 5th question has become "What will you do now?" We saw students not understand the intention to be future focused in their answers to the original 5th question: "How will you use that?" The answers are much more productive now that we have switched to the explicit assumption of future change: "What will you do now?"

We have expanded several other sections and added a new chapter about specific outcome—We Need an Outcome!

For those of you coming to *Open to Outcome, 2 Edition* from the first edition, we hope you enjoy the changes and find they make a difference in your teaching and facilitation.

Micah Jacobson
July, 2015

Introduction

"There is nothing so easy to learn as experience and nothing so hard to apply." —Josh Billings

Open to Outcome invites both new and experienced facilitators and teachers to explore and build effective methods for facilitating reflective discussions with groups. In particular, we want to introduce the model we call "The 5 Questions."

As trainers for the nationally recognized Link Crew and WEB orientation and transition programs*, and in a variety of other settings, we have many opportunities to work with students and educators using experiential activities and The 5 Questions. In every instance, the goal is to facilitate and explore the incredible potential of teaching and learning

---

* Link Crew and WEB are high school and middle school transition programs that train older students to become leaders and mentors for students in transition, usually 6th and 9th graders. The core methodology uses experience-based activities to train mentors to setup, facilitate, and lead reflection on the experiences created for the new students.

experientially. Like many of you, we have taken our share of bumps and bruises along the way. Fortunately, those experiences were balanced with incredible successes and powerful learning moments that continue to influence and shape our lives.

What have we learned, as facilitators, about the process of learning? First, we found that experiential learning engages students and educators in a way that is genuine and relevant. When people have an experience, whether in games, icebreakers, team-building exercises, simulations, initiatives, internships, or just in living life, opportunities exist to learn profound lessons. A skilled facilitator, asking the right questions and guiding reflective conversation before, during, and after an experience, can help open a gateway to powerful new thinking and learning.

Second, the process of questioning needed to achieve this powerful learning can be difficult to execute. We tried a variety of learning cycle approaches and found them either too conceptual for immediate application or too simple to create profound learning in the hands of moderately skilled facilitators.

This led us to create our own question model based on our beliefs about learning and learning cycles. The 5 Questions model is straightforward enough to teach high school students for immediate application, yet still comprehensive enough to allow facilitation of complex activities. It was always intended to be a starting place rather than a final destination in facilitation.

There are several ways to help participants process an experience. We have seen successful approaches that are learner-dependent like reflective writing or art, advanced techniques of questioning that are context and content specific, and a myriad of other techniques that can successfully turn experience into knowledge.

Like many of you, however, we needed an educator- or facilitator-dependent model that could be learned quickly and serve as an effective starting point in experiential learning. This has always been the objective of The 5 Questions model. As we developed this model, a number of other related concepts emerged that influenced how we work with groups and how we wrote this book.

The Basic Idea

The 5 Questions model and related methods explored in this book equip facilitators to guide participants toward internal reflection. Participants discover the learning that is true for them, not a predetermined outcome decided for them by the facilitator.

This is not to suggest this book and this model cannot be used within the context of traditional teaching with all the attendant outcome-based needs. In fact, thousands of teachers have reported using The 5 Questions with great success in the classroom. To account for this we have included a chapter on specific outcomes (see chapter five).

The challenge of being open to outcome is two-fold. The **first** challenge is for the facilitator to resist the temptation of imposing a particular learning and/or having a specific desired outcome for an activity. The **second** challenge is for the facilitator to remain open to the direction of the group's or individual's learning without losing focus of the experience and coming to no learning at all.

The more deeply the facilitator understands The 5 Questions model, the more skill the facilitator will have to bring participants back to the experience and guide them to reflect on what it means for them and what they can take from it.

How is This Approach Different?

Perhaps the greatest distinction of this model comes from the understanding and use of the verbs "to teach" and "to coach." These are complex verbs in the sense that each of them actually encompasses many other verbs within their definitions and they are often used interchangeably. For us, these two verbs are very distinct.

- **What is it to teach someone?** The fundamental definition of "teaching" is communicating new information. Talking, telling, lecturing, and demonstrating are some of the actions used in achieving this goal.

- **Alternatively, what is it to coach someone?** "Coaching," by our definition, is the process of reflecting on and expanding an idea or skill that has been previously learned.

In other words, once taught a piece of information or a skill, you can then be coached to develop thoughts about it or improve your ability to use it. The 5 Questions model supports the teaching/coaching process by providing a flexible structure for dialogue that facilitators can use to examine and reflect on an experience with groups or individuals. The ultimate goal is for each individual or group, through reflection and coaching, to realize a profound and unique learning that will modify their future behavior.

Why does this distinction between coaching and teaching matter in facilitation? Because facilitators, during the processing of an experience, should be doing more coaching and less teaching. They should be carefully observing participant behavior, guiding reflective conversation, and encouraging the application of what is learned. Beginning facilitators may slip unknowingly into teaching mode, telling participants what they should have learned (e.g., "This exercise was about teamwork"). The goal should be to help participants uncover the learning that is paramount for them. That means the fundamental tool of a facilitator should be questions rather than pre-determined answers.

Exploring The 5 Questions Model

In this book, we explain why we crafted each question, why we ask them in the order we ask them, and the mental mind-sets we use when we ask them.

In chapter one, we talk about learning. This chapter summarizes what we have discovered about how learning occurs. Using theoretical models by Kolb (1984) and Piaget (1976) to modern brain research, we attempt to highlight the critical pieces of how people actually learn.

In chapter two, we discuss the mental mind-sets that assist us in being the best facilitators possible. This chapter is about setting up dynamic reflective discussions in such a way that problems and challenges are prevented before they occur.

In chapter three, we give you The 5 Questions model. Each question is analyzed to help you understand why it was developed and what purpose it serves in moving the conversation forward to create powerful reflection and learning.

In chapter four, we outline strategies to keep the conversation moving. Of course, no amount of preventative work can anticipate every possibility. Chapter four is a toolkit for dealing with difficult issues and keeping a group on track.

In chapter five, we discuss adjustments and possibilities for using this model within the context of traditional outcome-based education. How can you bring students to learning while staying aware of the learning objectives that need to be met? We offer techniques and suggestions for guiding learning when necessary.

In chapter six, we present The 5 Questions model workshop we have given to educators, facilitators, and students over the years.

One Final Note: No process is foolproof. Although we continue to use and find success with our style and method of facilitating, please know we are not offering it as a panacea. We see The 5 Questions model and many of the other techniques in this book as tools rather than solutions. Tools work extremely effectively when used in the right way, in the right context, on the right problem. Trying to use a hammer when a saw is required will be frustrating for you and the hammer. We encourage you to pay attention to what works for you and what doesn't. Please let us know how it goes. We are eager to learn from you and will do what we can to help you become successful!

^{Chapter}_{One} | **What is Learning?**

"Learn your theories as well as you can, but put them aside when you touch the miracle of the living soul." —Carl Jung

The Quick-Start Guide to Human Understanding and Learning

The 5 Questions model is founded in both brain-based learning strategies and theories about facilitating experiences based on stages. Understanding the stages of learning will raise the potential for creating a more powerful facilitation of The 5 Questions.

A brief survey of everyone you know will most likely reveal that among the top five moments of learning in their lives, at least four did not take place in the classroom. The learning that really sticks, that comes to guide us in times of crisis, is learned through our own experiences. Micah can still vividly recall learning the satisfaction of sharing by getting the "best passer" award as a 6-year-old in AYSO soccer. Mari remembers her family moving across the country when she was in third grade. She learned the pain of saying good-bye for the first time when she left her childhood best friend, and she also learned the possibilities for new friends. You may recall memories of an experience that taught you a lesson you have never forgotten.

Learning is tricky. We learn a lot throughout our lives that we rarely use and even more that we have completely forgotten. Then there are those learning moments that stand out as pivotal—when you learn a lesson that forever remains with you. Think about yourself for a moment. Who taught you about kindness? What did that experience look like? What about learning the value of money? How did you come to see its importance (or lack of importance) in your life?

When Micah was 10, his mother gave him a $20 bill and sent him to the grocery store on his bike. Somehow on the way to the store, it slipped out of his pocket. He knew it was a big deal, but was not prepared for the search his mother made him undertake. Together they searched each grain of sand between their house and the grocery store. They never did find the money; however, Micah never forgot the search. He came to understand they searched hard because to his mom, money was very important and was not something to be taken lightly. A completely different learning would have occurred if Micah's mother had simply shrugged it off and taken him back to the grocery store. Each experience in our lives has the potential to leave an imprint, shaping the way we view, exist in, and interact with the world.

The term "experiential learning" can be applied to everything from on-the-job training to structured simulations in a workshop environment. It could be argued that everything that happens in our lives is ultimately an experience. However, we believe it is important to differentiate experiential learning from abstract text learning or lecture-based learning. While it is possible to use The 5 Questions methodology with those modes of learning (see chapter five), we are specifically writing for facilitators and teachers who use simulations, initiatives, games, and activities in the classroom and want to process those experiences with their students. Our approach is not a comprehensive educational tool and by necessity must be complemented by other teaching and processing tools.

The idea that we learn through experience is a very old one. Aristotle wrote "for the things we have to learn before we can do them, we learn by doing them." The old adage reminds us that "experience is the best teacher." However, a careful examination of that thought reveals it can't be completely true; because we have many experiences that teach us nothing.

We build on the proposition laid down in the early 20th century by John Dewey: People can construct knowledge through their own experience. Dewey had a significant impact on education as an advocate of learning through experience and practical experimentation. He established a different lens through which educators might view their teaching choices:

> "... to imposition from above is opposed free activity; to learning from texts and teachers, learning through experience; to acquisition of isolated skills and techniques by drill is opposed acquisition of them as means of attaining ends which make direct vital appeal; to preparation for a more or less remote future is opposed making the most of the opportunities to present life; to static aims and materials is opposed acquaintance with a changing world ..." (Dewey, 1938, p. 19)

We are interested in how the experiences of life get translated into learning. Why do some people permanently change their outlook on life after experiencing an outdoor challenge or classroom simulation, while others quickly return to their same habits and beliefs?   *make structure work for you*

These variables occur because the learning that results from experience is often unstructured. For example, people may draw different conclusions from getting their first speeding ticket. For one, it is a lesson in safer, more controlled driving. For another, it is further proof crying doesn't work nearly as well as reputed. For a third person, the experience never enters long-term memory and little of it is actually stored. The complex arrangement of brain neurochemistry, genetics, emotional state, prior experience, and other influences combine in each moment to create learning.

What are some things we do know about how we learn? Understanding how people learn turns out to be an incredibly difficult challenge. The actual path of acquiring new knowledge touches on many different places in the brain, depending on the content and context of the learning. Only a few aspects of the process seem clear:

- Learning begins before consciousness and is ongoing in people with normal brain function.
- People learn the most when they want to learn.
- People learn from experience.
- People learn from conceptual forms and ideas.
- Stages of cognitive and emotional development are loosely related to learning.

(Brookfield, 1986, p. 25-30)

The Science of the Brain

Brain research in the last 30 years has exploded many of our previously held notions of how the brain works. Most importantly, we have learned we are creating new brain cells throughout our lives. The brain is highly adaptable even at advanced ages, suggesting old dogs can, in fact, learn new tricks. This is not to say adult learning is easy. Brain "excitation" and growth are in hyper-drive in childhood, peaking for girls around age eleven and for boys around age fourteen (Jensen, 2015). With that said, dramatic and important learning continues to happen throughout the teenage years and all through adulthood. It may not happen quite as rapidly but it is absolutely still happening. A review of what happens as the brain develops will help shed light on how we can use an understanding of brain neurochemistry to help the groups with which we work learn more effectively.

We are born with somewhere around 200 billion neurons. Rather than being a blank slate upon which the world will write a personality, these neurons represent a sort of cumulative possibility function, the components of which include genes, fetal environment, nourishment, and the mother's emotional state. During the first few years of life, experience helps connect these neurons to each other. Those that are used and connected join together rapidly while those that are not used eventually fall away.

By about age three, we have cut our original gift of neurons in half to about 100 billion. At this point, "a kind of irreversibility" sets in. "There is this shaping process that goes on early, and then at the end of this process, be that age two, three, or four, you have essentially designed a brain that probably is not going to change very much more" (Kotulak, 1996, p. 7). At this point, those remaining 100 billion neurons have made an average of 10,000 connections. The connected neurons are able to form neural pathways that represent learning and memory. Our brains are able to ask and answer questions like, "What is an orange? What happens when I throw it? What did the last orange I ate taste like?"

Interestingly, these neural connections don't just wait around. Although the "gray matter" or basic neuronal structure of the brain is in place in early childhood, the "white matter" or connections between neurons is only just getting started (Jensen, 2015). The brain wants to be constantly exposed to new and different experiences. "Unless the brain is continuously challenged, it loses some of the connections that grew out of a college experience. The brains of university graduates who led mentally inactive lives had fewer connections than those of graduates who never stopped letting the light in" (Kotulak, 1996, p. 18).

How Does the Brain Learn?

The brain learns by taking in sensory data and then labeling, categorizing, and connecting that data to previously stored information. In the broadest sense, the brain learns everything through experience. By experience here we mean the broadest possible definition of sensation: everything we see, hear, touch, taste, and smell. The more neural connections are reinforced through repeated experience, include multisensory stimulation, and involve emotional stake, the greater the likelihood the information will be retained.

Confucius knew what modern MRI scans now confirm: "Tell me and I'll forget; show me and I'll understand; involve me and I'll remember." This correlates with the work done in the 1960s by the National Training Laboratories of Bethel, Maine (now the NTL Institute of Alexandria, Virginia). They studied the percentage of new learning students retained after 24 hours of being taught by a particular teaching method. Their data showed after lecture and reading techniques, students retained only 5% and 10% of the new information. By contrast, when the technique used was practice by doing or teaching others, the retention rate shot up to 75% and 90% respectively (Sousa, p. 95).

Using What We Know

We know we should make experience multisensory, and we should encourage reflection and conscious processing of information. The challenge then is to use this information moment by moment in a processing session.

Jean Piaget (1976) offers an excellent starting place for understanding what we do with new information. Piaget developed the concepts of assimilation and accommodation. Simply stated, these processes involve learning from either external stimuli or from internal thought processes.

Accommodation occurs when we adapt our view of the world to new sensory information. We see something new. This new experience is brought into the set of information we previously held, and we adjust our internal notions to accommodate this new information.

Assimilation occurs when new stimulus fits into already established mental constructs. We experience a beautiful sunrise and file it into the mental category of beautiful experiences. We assimilate this new experience into an already existing set of beliefs.

As experiential facilitators and educators, we can imagine participants struggling to place their experience. They alternate through different aspects of assimilating the experience into connections already established and accommodating their beliefs to make room for this new data. When we, as facilitators, understand this process, we can ask questions and offer support as they assimilate and accommodate.

Stages to Learning

David Kolb wrote one of the basic experiential learning texts, *Experiential Learning*, in 1984. Kolb noted the ways in which we grasp sensory data and transform it into knowledge. He combined the experiential philosophy of John Dewey, the cognitive developmental psychology of Jean Piaget, and the social psychology and action research contributions of Kurt Lewin (1947) to create a model of learning. Kolb spoke of four learning paradigms or stages (see figure 1:1). Each stage is related to the others, and all are necessary for important, long-lasting, and meaningful learning.

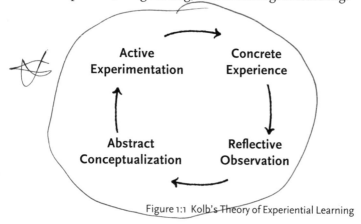

Figure 1:1 Kolb's Theory of Experiential Learning

Kolb argued that different individuals process information and learn in terms of a dominant tendency in one of the above stages. For Kolb, these were not necessarily linear stages in a learning process, but rather, connected processes individuals may or may not use to learn.

How can we use this understanding of learning to help develop and facilitate learning experiences? When you have this knowledge, you can guide your participants to their own "aha" moments. "Aha" moments are the moments educators live for. They happen when someone finally puts the pieces of a lesson together and molds them into a comprehensive understanding or belief that then becomes part of his/her life.

Micah experienced such a moment when conducting a Link Crew orientation where the seniors and juniors were serving as mentors/facilitators for the incoming freshmen. At one point, the mentors took their groups on a tour of the campus. Micah had stopped in the restroom to wash his hands when a freshman boy came running in. Taking no notice of Micah, the boy began to fill a water gun. Micah had specifically asked the leaders not to use water guns on their tour, so he suspected this freshman was out to cause a little trouble.

Rather than take a traditional command-and-control approach, Micah tried to create a learning opportunity with the following conversation.

Micah: Hey, what's going on?
Freshman: (swiftly hiding gun) Uh, nothing.
Micah: What are you doing with the water gun?
Freshman: (gun hanging down at his side) Uh, nothing ... oh, my leader asked me to fill this.

Micah: Wow, you've only known me for a few moments and you may have already lied to me. How does that feel?
Freshman: What?
Micah: I asked the leaders not to use water guns, so it is possible you are lying to me. Why did you do that?
Freshman: Uh, I don't know.
Micah: Is that something you do all the time? Lie to people you just met?
Freshman: Well, no. I mean, I guess. Uh, am I in trouble?
Micah: What do you think should happen now?
Freshman: I guess I should give you the gun, right?
Micah: Sure, if you think that's the right thing to do. What would you do differently next time?
Freshman: Well, I guess I should stay with my group.
Micah: Okay, sounds good.

Micah kept asking the boy questions that might get him to reflect on his actions. It was Micah's hope that as the boy reflected on his concrete experiences, he might begin to understand more productive ways of behaving and come to his own answers—experience his own "aha."

Of course this situation is not quite the same as a facilitator with a group. Micah represented an authority figure and the boy just wanted to get out of the way as quickly and painlessly as possible. Still, what might he have thought or learned if Micah had simply said, "Hey, you're not supposed to have water guns; hand it over!"

Constructivism

The model of learning just described is often associated with a constructivist paradigm. The constructivist school of thought has a rich tradition, and like any school of thought it is not without critique. Critics claim this theory places too much emphasis on the cognitive processes, ignores subconscious and psychic ways of learning, and places emphasis on the individual while de-emphasizing the cultural and contextual aspects of learning.

What is learning from a constructivist point of view? Essentially individuals are constantly constructing knowledge based on their experience of the world. Constructivism asserts an individual's interactions with his/her environment produces specific observations, which are then interpreted and generalized into concepts of the way the world works. These concepts are then called knowledge and used in future settings to guide behavior and feeling. This cycle then repeats as new experiences yield new observations, which are furthered processed into new ideas for application.

You've Got a Stage, I've Got a Question

There have been many before us who proposed a cycle of questions to promote learning. Both of us were initially introduced to a form of questioning that roughly follows the Pfeiffer and Jones (1975) 5 Stage model (see figure 1:2). However, like other highly conceptual models, the Pfeiffer and Jones model is difficult for some to understand and challenging to master in a short period of time.

The simplicity of Outward Bound's "What? So What? Now What?" and James Neill's "Do, Review, Plan" is appealing, but it is difficult to achieve a consistent application of the process by a variety of facilitators. Although they are easy to remember, the challenge of really addressing each learning stage involved in processing the experience remains. Often simple models fail to adequately address what we see as the

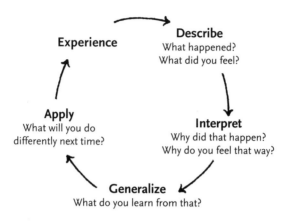

Figure 1:2 Adapted Pfeiffer and Jones 5 Stage Model

critical interpretation stage (i.e., asking "What?" then "Why?" before moving to "So What?").

Follow-up questions are another approach to facilitating experience. These are a list of specific questions related to the activity. Participants generally either connect directly to the questions, resulting in a successful discussion, or more commonly, a deafening silence follows as you work to make the group think about the specific issues raised by the question. These issues may or may not resonate with the participants' experience. Practically, it is also awkward to hold a list of questions in your hand as you facilitate.

How The 5 Questions Model Fits In

The 5 Questions model rests on the foundation of brain research, stage theory of learning, and a constructivist paradigm. They are the theories behind the model. We want you to know this because the simplicity of each question is at first deceptive! And to be the most effective facilitator you can be, we want you to have all the background you can. Before we proceed, there are two more ideas to consider about learning: "framing the experience" and "emotional stake."

Framing the Experience

The philosophy of The 5 Questions model is one of being "open to outcome," which is to be open to the learning that can emerge from the individuals and the group. This does not preclude having learning objectives. In every learning situation, a good facilitator will always be thinking about the objectives of the experience. You might even have possible learning scenarios in mind. For example, when teaching a lesson on the Civil War, you may want students to learn about specific economic factors that provided the subtext for the conflict around slavery. In a workgroup low-ropes course, a facilitator may hope colleagues face some of their conflicting behaviors and maybe even come to see they can successfully overcome them. You are not at cross purposes with being open to outcome if you come into the learning environment with objectives centered around your hopes for the experience at hand. These objectives help the participants frame their experience.

How do you successfully frame an experience and remain open? Your objectives should focus on the process rather than the content. This means considering **how** the group learns and the quality of the learning environment. It does not mean deciding exactly **what** the group will learn. In fact, it most likely means not knowing what the group will learn but remaining open to what that learning could be.

- **How then can your objectives best be achieved?** Focus on keeping objectives behavioral and cognitive in scope rather than content-directed. For example, when facilitating a workshop on diversity, rather than orient yourself toward a particular leaning, i.e., "We are a judgmental species and participants must change their own internal stereotypes," focus instead on the quality of the experience, i.e., "Participants will have the opportunity to look closely at their own biases and engage in an honest dialogue about them."

The Notion of Stake

So the experience went really well and yet it seemed participants learned nothing. This dilemma brings us to another point on the nature of learning—the notion of "stake."

- **What is stake?** Think of it as the emotional or cognitive risk that participants feel. In general, the more emotional stake invested in the experience, the more powerful the learning opportunity. This is not to say if you have nothing at stake you can't learn anything. Sometimes powerful learning can happen simply by watching from the sidelines; however, the potential of actually being in the game and having something to lose makes learning much more probable.

Imagine attending a retreat with a group of relative strangers. The facilitator asks for volunteers to demonstrate an important concept and, being adventurous, you raise your hand and step forward. How much do you have at risk in this moment? What if we replace the group of strangers with your closest friends? What about work colleagues? How does your thinking about participating in this experiment change based on who is observing?

Now, imagine the experiment involves hypnosis. The facilitator makes no mention of what kinds of activities you are going to undergo. Are you nervous yet? Some people might not be if they feel safe in the situation or maybe have a limited fear of embarrassment. For others, their hearts are starting to beat faster just reading about it. As your emotional stake rises, the possibility for a long-term "learning" increases. Interestingly, as you might no-doubt imagine, we tend to learn more from extreme negative experiences than we do from extreme positive ones. If the facilitator were to proceed and embarrass you, many people might decide then and there never to volunteer again. Others might begin to establish parameters for their participation. Compare that with the persons who felt minimal emotional stake in the experience. Embarrassed or not, they are unlikely to change their behavior in the future. They simply carry on as before.

The reason emotional stake matters so much lies in a little almond-shaped part of the brain called the amygdala. The amygdala processes a great majority of our emotional reactions and is intimately tied to our cortex, the processing part of our brain. The memories we ultimately store have an emotional connection to the amygdala. That means just about everything we learn has an emotional overlay. We don't just "know" things, we feel and know things simultaneously.

It's Just a Game

If you work with young people, you have probably heard "this is just a game" a million times. They believe because this is just a game, they don't have to care about it, and their behavior ultimately doesn't matter. This is the game they are playing with themselves so they won't have to learn anything. They are saying to themselves, "If it is just a game to me, then I have no stake in the outcome, and I don't need to reflect on what I said or did." As a facilitator with any group, you can raise the stakes involved simply by helping people see they are always somewhat at risk.

Micah presented a simulation to highlight experiences in win-win or win-lose situations with a group in Southern California. People had the opportunity to lie or cheat in order to win, and many groups opt for those behaviors. With Micah's particular group a lot of lying and cheating had gone on, which enabled one team to win "the game" easily. When the other group brought this up, the winning group smiled and said, "It doesn't matter if we lied; this was just a game and the point was to win, which we did." They didn't feel enough personal, emotional involvement in the experience to allow learning to occur.

Micah asked them to reflect on themselves in and out of the experience. "Do you typically lie or cheat in your lives? When do you find that helpful? When does it hurt? When did you decide it was okay to do so in this experience? Did you stop being yourselves while you were playing today? Did you become someone else?" Micah raised the stakes by having them look closer and acknowledge accountability for their behavior. His questions allowed the group to look at their own patterns of interaction and ultimately at the patterns at work in the world around them. When you raise the emotional stakes, you increase the potential for learning.

Too Much at Stake

There is the potential to raise the stakes too high in a simulated environment. Just like having nothing at stake, when participants have too much at stake, they are also at risk of shutting themselves off to learning and moving instead into a survival mode. This can happen when individuals are singled out in an unsupportive environment. A "fight or flight" instinct engages, and extreme resistance can quickly build up. This creates blocks to learning that are impossible to overcome. When this is the situation, it is best to lower the stakes. Look for ways to take the focus away from particular individuals and ask potentially less threatening questions. It doesn't serve the group or the facilitator to force learning into a situation that is not ready for it.

We can also raise the emotional stakes too high by creating an overly stressed environment. We get stressed when we feel threatened, and the brain makes little distinction between real or imagined threat. When in a highly threatening environment, our brain shuts learning off even more than in low emotional stake environments. We no longer have the ability to see the world clearly or process new information (Jensen, 2008).

Getting It Just Right

In the end, it is a balancing act. Figure 1:3 shows the balance between not enough and too much at stake. There is a fine line between not enough and too much emotional or cognitive investment for an environment to lend itself to learning experiences. Facilitators stand a better chance of creating incredible learning opportunities when focusing on some of the fundamentals of effective facilitation like creat-

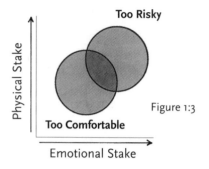

Figure 1:3

ing a supportive and productive environment, encouraging supportive and reflective dialogue, and checking your own agenda at the door.

Some people think of this as it relates to three zones: the comfort zone, the learning zone, and the panic zone. Figure 1:3 distinguishes between the three areas with additional risk being added as you move out either axis.

Putting It All Together

Understanding how learning occurs and what enhances or hinders learning will make you a better facilitator. As you think about your role in the group, consider the concepts of a learning cycle, brain-based learning, learning objectives, and emotional stake to set up a framework for how you might philosophically approach your task. We constantly learn more on these topics. Participants, colleagues, and our own experiences of being facilitated continue to provide a practical backdrop to the theories we hold to be true. Ultimately, a theory is only as good as its ability to provide useful explanation and prediction of actual occurrence. Additionally, theory alone is rarely useful. Part of the motivation for writing this book was a belief that we could make practical some of the theoretical underpinnings of reflecting on experiences. The next few chapters aim to do just that.

Creating Space and the Facilitator Mind-Set

"In teaching, it is the method and not the content that is the message ... the drawing out, not the pumping in."

—Ashley Montague

When a group gathers for the purpose of learning from a shared experience, it is common and often helpful for someone to step into the role of facilitator. For our purposes, this can look like a teacher in the classroom, a facilitator on a ropes course, or a troop leader at a scout meeting. Ideally, a facilitator's role is to assist the group and group members in discovering their own learning. A facilitator presupposes the group will have all the answers. The job of the facilitator is to make the process easier. That's not to say the process will be easy every step of the way, as it often is not. It does mean it is the task of the facilitator to tend to the process.

This chapter describes the most important things to consider before you begin asking questions of the group and reflecting on the experience. When facilitators pay attention to these items and adopt these mental mind-sets, group members consistently go deeper into their own profound learning. There are wonderful resources for learning to facilitate, many of which are listed in our references. This chapter is meant to highlight the most compelling and practical aspects of creating space and getting into a helpful mind-set for facilitation.

Creating Space

The first consideration we make when designing a learning experience is the physical space. It can help or hurt. It can make the group more or less comfortable. It is **part** of the group and the experience. You can and **should** be aware of the physical space as it will dramatically impact your success. Once you make the mental shift to believe this concept, it will be difficult not to notice the quality of the spaces in which you find yourself. "How will people feel in this space? How will it protect or create comfort for the inhabitants? How will the space support the activity?" As an architect uses windows, doors, and walls to affect the room, facilitators move furniture and arrange bodies in order to impact the experience of the conversation that will take place.

Working predominantly in schools, we have our share of challenging spaces. We have conducted trainings in libraries and cafeterias, on football fields and in science labs. Every time we walk into a new space we try to imagine the group interacting within the space. Where will everyone sit? What distractions are present? What might get in the way? Do everything you can to rearrange the room to suit your purposes.

Remember as a student the allure of "going outside." On a nice warm day, students may beg a teacher, "Let's do this lesson outside!" This doesn't change at all when working with adults by the way. When conducting professional development for educators and administrators, we are asked to go outside all the time. On very few occasions, the space, intention, and time of an experience actually make going outside a better choice. What a great day, right?! For the most part, however, unless the day is structured to be outside (as in a challenge course), going outside is more of a distraction than an asset. Why is that? Generally, it is because you lose the container for the shared experience a room provides and introduce a host of additional distractions. As a facilitator, you must manage the space and give yourself permission to construct it in a way that works for you, including potentially saying no to requests to change the space.

Ideally, a group will reflect in the same space used to conduct the experience. If the space itself is too distracting, then the closest appropriate space will have to work.

What would be the *best* setup for group reflection? The space should be large enough to accommodate all group members seated in a circle with no furniture or other items in the middle of the circle. If the group will be talking for a while, everyone should have a comfortable chair. Or, if group members are flexible enough, they could sit on the floor or ground. When seated, everyone should be able to see everyone else. The facilitator should be part of the circle at the same physical level as the participants (i.e., everyone seated or everyone standing).

The position you take indicates your relationship to the group. Teachers stand in front of the class. Colleagues gather around a table. Leaders sit at the head of the table. Friends sit with each other. Where do you put yourself? If you stand in front, you have immediately created some physical separation between you and the group.

Mari watched as a high school student attempted to lead a group of her peers in reflection. The student stood up front as she imagined a leader should. The group sat scattered in desks as she attempted to get them to answer her processing questions. The group largely ignored her. Later the student leader commented that her group "sucked." Mari asked her to reflect on how she had positioned herself relative to the rest of the group. Did she notice how students rolled their eyes even before she started the debrief? Did she see how standing in front of them might have sent a message that she thought she was better than the group? Slowly she came to understand the power of levels and seating. Such a simple thing, yet it can make or break an experience.

Additional things to consider when creating the space:

- What interruptions might occur, and how can they be handled?
- Where is the bathroom, so you can tell participants?
- Will people be coming in once you've started? How will you welcome them into the conversation?
- Is the temperature in the room or outside where you are sitting too hot or too cold?
- Can everyone hear everyone else?
- Are there any random, annoying noises, or visuals to distract group members? If so, can you adjust things to avoid these?

Create your own checklist. Refer to it as you consider the space for your next facilitation in order to create better opportunities for success.

When moving from the space where the experience happened to the space where reflection will occur, work to create the new space swiftly and with as much flow as possible so group members don't even notice you're tending to the space. This means, if at all possible, consider the physical space before the experience occurs. Move the furniture and adjust the temperature before people arrive. Have a plan for breaks. Make sure there is adequate space. If **you** think about it, then they won't have to. Instead, their attention can be on the conversation and the learning.

Circle Up!

Forming a circle is the most ancient and powerful way for a group to symbolically be in an egalitarian relationship to one another. Making time to form a circle is well worth the effort because conversation flows more easily when everyone is at the same physical level and can see everyone else. Circles by their very nature invite everyone to participate. A circle helps bring the shy or quiet ones into the process and, because there is no stage, it tends to calm the loud and showy ones. In a circle, the facilitator can more easily guide the process.

Some groups may resist forming a circle. It could be because they don't want to be that intimate with one another, and circles are intimate. Or perhaps they don't want to be held accountable to one another. Another common reason groups won't easily move into a circle is they just don't have much practice at it. In any of these circumstances, it's best to use a little humor and grace while simply insisting upon and expecting cooperation. If you have chairs, it helps to have them placed in a circle.

While facilitating a group of school administrators, Mari had one particularly resistant participant. This person chose a chair several feet away from the circle and slightly turned, as if to physically indicate his unwillingness to join the conversation as an equal. Mari gathered the rest of the group and quietly whispered instructions. The group members simultaneously picked up their chairs and moved to form a circle including this gentleman. He sat there stunned. As the group took their seats, never saying a word directly to him, he finally laughed and said, "Okay, okay, I get it." He then turned his chair in and became a willing and valuable contributor to the conversation. Over and over, we have seen circling the group together from the beginning make an incredible difference. Sometimes gentle nudging is required.

The Facilitator Mind-Set—Genuine Curiosity

As the facilitator, you are acting as a conduit for the participants; therefore, your internal mind-set has a definite impact on them. If you remember or do nothing else as a facilitator, remember this: show genuine curiosity about the participants and their experience, and profound learning will emerge.

- **How would you define "genuine"?** Synonyms for genuine are authentic, real, and true. It is not fake, false, or imitation. Think of someone you know who is genuine and likely you will smile and feel a connection in your heart. That is the power of being genuine.

- We have seen a number of people facilitate the way they think they are supposed to—using the right words and gestures. It is like they are playing the role of "facilitator" rather than being genuinely curious. How can you find the person within you that is not wearing any masks? Who are you? How do you bring that person to your facilitation?

Now consider the definition of "curiosity." To wonder, to explore, to be engaged, to feel your mind awake—this is curiosity. When was the last time you were passionately curious? Can you remember a time when you were so curious that questions kept rumbling in your mind? What sparked that curiosity? How did you feed it? Do you notice the difference between times of great curiosity and times of boredom?

How do you combine the two concepts? Really think about the two together; let yourself be **genuinely curious** about the participants with whom you are working. From where have they come? What does this experience mean for them? What possibilities exist? Let yourself be genuinely curious about the potential lessons embedded in your experience together? What patterns were present? What surprised you? Where did you see conflict?

To help evoke a state of genuine curiosity, try to recall yourself at five. Think about the intense curiosity and interest in the world of a 5-year-old you know. Put yourself in the vortex of that curiosity. When that 5-year-old asks a question, his/her entire self seeks the answer, and when the answer comes, another question immediately arises. The questions and answers tumble together in the delight of discovery. As a facilitator, your challenge is to call forth that state of curiosity and delight.

Lessons From Improv Comedy

In addition to genuine curiosity, we have found three concepts from the world of improvisational comedy or improv to be invaluable for remaining open to outcome when facilitating a group reflection.

- **What is improv?** It is a form of theatre in which the actors, known as players, act within a given format. Because they are only given an outline or a set of rules, all the words and movements are not practiced in advance. They must improvise in the moment. This is akin to what facilitators of experiential activities do. There is a structure, but we never know exactly what we will need to do or say. As prepared as you may be, every group brings something different to the experience.

Excellent improv players operate from three intertwined beliefs about the process, their fellow players, the audience, and the set. They are **yes/and, go big,** and **total support**.

We have borrowed these concepts and lay no claim to having created them. Both of us have studied improv in a variety of settings, and we have deep appreciation for professional improv players. We are not them. What we have done with great success is take the principles of improv and adapt them to help new facilitators become increasingly skilled. By thinking and playing with these three concepts, facilitation students have generated powerful insights. Each of these beliefs runs counter in some way to the general cultural milieu. They require some level of careful study and are helped by constant reinforcement.

Beyond simply helping with facilitation, having now lived with and taught these concepts for more than 15 years, we can say with confidence they are also philosophies of life. While deceptively simple to learn and understand, living out these concepts in daily life is a practice that can, over time, change your life in immeasurable ways. These three philosophies are game changers, not just in facilitation, but also in life.

Yes/And

The goal of each improv player, and in our case each facilitator, is to keep the scene engaging and moving forward. Therefore, players build on and contribute to what has happened in the scene, taking the story-line in a new and creative direction. In facilitation, this means the facilitator builds on, probes for depth, and encourages group members to inquire from themselves and fellow group members about what is being discussed.

What does an engaging environment look like? Recall those times when you have been with friends or colleagues and it seemed as if every idea built on those that came before. Although not every idea was acted on or even seen as good, every idea seemed to have a place because it helped lead to the next one—and the next idea might be brilliant.

How does yes/and change the response? The opposite of **yes/and** is **no/but** or **yes/but**. Think of a time you enthusiastically shared an idea with someone who responded with, "That's a great idea, but what about ...?" The "but" in the response has the effect of letting the air out of your enthusiasm balloon. In improv, that's known as a block. The person with the idea has to use extra energy to overcome the block, energy that could be used to be more creative and because it's comedy, more funny. In life, when we hear "**yes, but** ...," it deflates us. We have to use extra energy to overcome the block and re-inflate—energy that could be used in getting to the next brilliant idea.

When we deliberately change our language or thought process to **yes/and** and really mean it, people open up and get more into their ideas. Notice the subtle and powerful shift in this response to your enthusiasm and your idea: "That's a great idea, and what about...." **Yes/and** opens up the pathway to synergy and tremendous potential.

J P does this well

Look at the following dialogue as an example:

Jeff: I wish we had more instructions before we played. I felt like you didn't tell us what we were doing so we didn't really have a chance to succeed!

Facilitator: Yes, and what did you do with the instructions I did give?

Jeff: Well, we tried to understand them, but we wasted a lot of time wondering what we could and could not do. It was never made clear.

Facilitator: I saw that too (Yes). Was time spent wondering the best use of your time, especially considering everyone got the same unclear instructions (And)?

Notice that saying yes/and does not have to mean actually using the words "yes," "and." It is really more a way of thinking about the present moment than a use of language. One way to think about **yes/and** is to break it down. "Yes" refers to acknowledgement—not necessarily agreement—that what someone said was true for him or her in that moment. It is a way of saying, "Yes, you did just say that" or "Yes, that really did just happen." This lets the person know they were heard rather than immediately dismissed. Starting the sentence with "but" or "no" is a denial of what they said and can lead some to believe they were not truly heard in the first place.

"And" is additive; it moves the conversation forward by adding what is true or unique for you. For instance, a friend wants to see a movie. You are hungry. Rather than shutting down your friend, you can acknowledge his/her desire and then add your perspective: "Yes, and it would be great to get something to eat, because I'm really hungry right now." "And" enables you to have a place in the conversation and to keep it moving forward without having to simply agree with what others are saying.

Yes/and is more about a mind-set than the actual language. You can easily **no/but** someone with the words **yes/and**. Look at the following dialogue:

> Calvin: I was thinking that as a group we should have taken some time to plan more at the beginning.
>
> Angela: Yes, and that is exactly what you always say!

In this example, Angela uses the words **yes/and**, but her meaning and intention is still to put up a block for Calvin. To really understand the spirit of acknowledgement and addition takes some practice.

What about difficult or hostile situations? Can you use **yes/and** when someone makes a racial slur or publicly demeans another group member? These can be some of the most powerful moments for a group and must be handled carefully. Think of how different responses will impact the group. A comment like, "It is not appropriate to say things like that in this group," is certainly understandable and sometimes advisable and has a very specific reaction. It shuts down further communication. This may not always be the right choice. What might happen if you simply answered, "Yes, and how is it that you have come to believe such a hurtful thing?" Still laden with judgment, this sentence allows for a continuation of the dialogue. Even less judgmental would be a simple question: "Why do you believe that?" Whatever your style, holding to the concept of **yes/and**, even when it is difficult, can be transformative for the group and also for you.

Micah received a thank you note from a 7th grade teacher that went something like this:

> *I was really skeptical about the potential of yes/and during the training. However, when we got home, I realized I had the perfect test case. One of my 3rd period students has been difficult and taxing all year. It feels like I often spend half the class period telling him "no" in one way or another. "Put your hand down." "No, you may not go to the bathroom." "Could you please keep your hands to yourself." I decided that I would challenge myself to spend one period trying to just say yes/and. I'll admit it was an incredible challenge. I was pretty exhausted by the end of that day. However, I was AMAZED when the very next day turned into the easiest of the entire year. He simply didn't try to make my life difficult at every turn. It was almost like when I stopped telling him no, the game wasn't interesting to him anymore and he lost the energy for it! THANK YOU! I will forever believe in the power of yes/and.*

How do you keep "yes/and" in the front of your mind? The **first** technique is simply to write in big letters, on whatever notes you may use, "YES, AND." Seeing the words as you facilitate calls to mind the belief. The **second** technique is to stay constantly aware of your own emotional state. If you feel yourself tightening and resisting a group or a particular person's energy, mentally go through a process of what would happen if you could say

yes/and in that situation. How might you respond differently if you didn't try so hard to resist? A **third** technique is to appoint a colleague to monitor your words. Have them note your responses to the group and later review when you had a yes/and response and when you had a no/but response. By becoming increasingly aware of your responses, you will gain the power to yes/and whenever you want.

Go Big

The idea of **go big** is to show up fully in your presence with the group. For an improv player, it means to move past the fear of doing or saying the wrong thing, and instead trust the dynamic flow of the scene. For a facilitator, it means to be fully present with the group and trust the process and your skills as a facilitator. To both an improv player and a facilitator it means daring to be outrageous or quiet. Trust what you say and do will be the right thing, and if it isn't, even that will be the right thing.   *self · reliance*

It is also important to consider what **go big** is not. It is not monopolizing the conversation. It is not jumping around and being a cheerleader. **Go big** is not about upstaging your group or giving them the answers. It has nothing at all to do with how "big" physically or vocally you are.

Go big means to be alert and aware with every cell of your mental and physical being. Refuse to be small. Say "no" to the parts of you that critique and judge and second-guess. The world is already in too much pain for any of us to act small or hold back. What you do makes a difference for others. **Go big** says the difference you make will be big. Use your skills and talents to the maximum of your ability. Do not let any person or group make you feel small. As Marianne

Williamson (1996) so eloquently wrote in her book *A Return to Love: Reflections on the Principles of a Course in Miracles,* "Our deepest fear is not that we are inadequate. Our deepest fear is that we are powerful beyond measure ... As we are liberated from our own fear, our presence automatically liberates others."

Adopting a **go big** mind-set enables you to take risks. You can go where the group needs you to go and say what the group needs you to say. Actors refer to this as "committing to the moment." In a facilitation moment this might mean calling out a particular behavior. *Permission to fail*

Mari was facilitating a group of high school students through a low ropes set of initiatives. The group was generally not engaging at its highest potential. At one point, a student commented that they were tired of playing these stupid games. Mari's heart sank; the students had been negative all day, and she was tired. She sat quietly for a minute and then decided to **go big**. Mari looked directly at the student and quietly responded, "Do you notice you are constantly playing games?" For some reason this was the right question to ask. Group members got serious for the first time. They thought deeply about the kinds of games people play with others and with themselves. Not only was it a profound conversation, but the entire group became much more interactive. Looking back, it may not seem like a great risk. However, in that moment, Mari knew she was going big.

- Can you go big and not get your ego wrapped up in your success? Can you go big and say nothing at all? Can you go big and have the ability to acknowledge that the next time you can do it even better? **Go big** holds two things as true: **First**, you are

capable of being there for your group in a way that will manifest
profound change. **Second**, it is not entirely about you. Holding
both these beliefs at the same time can make your facilitation
ascend to a more effective level.

Total Support $\xi \angle A$!

Total support means standing with your people. It is the
mind-set that exclaims, "I am here for us!" In improv, **total
support** means moving through a scene in such a way that
each player looks as good as possible. If one player is center
stage, the other players move and behave in ways to make
the focal person look as good as possible.

Very clearly **total support** means never demeaning, belit-
tling, or humiliating someone in the group. For some of us,
the temptation to be negatively sarcastic or to put people "in
their place" rises up easily. How can you support a group
and dismiss them at the same time? You can't.

Sarcasm is interesting, as it shows up in many different
places, often even with some mild intention of being supportive. Rarely is it. The word "sarcasm" originally comes from a
Greek word, "sarkazein" which means, "to tear at the flesh."
Sarcasm gets its roots from violence and the use of it today
retains that abrasive quality. The sarcastic person creates a
layer of safety between self and victims—"Yeah, I'll get that
to you right away." Because the intended meaning is exactly
opposite of the spoken words, the sarcastic person makes the
listener his/her victim by not allowing that person to really
question him/her. Acting with Total Support doesn't mean
never being sarcastic, but it does mean becoming aware of
the amount of sarcasm used and the intended victims.

- **What does it mean to facilitate with total support?** Extend a strong, permeating energy of support through everything: yourself, the group, what is being said, where the conversation is heading. Believe in what is happening, and support the people and the conversation. Look out for everyone all at once and with equal attention. When you operate from this place, group members will begin to feel **total support**. As total support builds in a group, people begin to trust themselves and one another, resulting in more creativity, depth, and risk-taking.

Total support does not mean surrendering yourself, because an important part of **total support** is supporting yourself, too. You cannot allow yourself to be demeaned or belittled by the group any more than you would allow group members to do that to each other. You are not supporting the group or yourself by letting one participant dominate.

To that end, total support is definitely not the same thing as total agreement. Total support includes supporting yourself and your integrity. It is absolutely not total support to simply agree with someone in order to avoid conflict. Total support sometimes means questioning authority and holding people accountable. If you are acting with your own sense of integrity, aware of what is happening around you, and offering your own contribution (see **go big**), then you are in total support.

The Challenges of Total Support

Facilitators constantly struggle with when to move a conversation forward. People like to rehash moments and ideas. It is tough to move away from a comment that stirs several people to contribute. Even when the group does move away from a topic, some participants demand to move backward so their perspectives can be heard. You don't have to facilitate long to understand that groups can cycle. Many facilitators feel they have to ensure every person is heard. The question to ask is whether allowing everyone to be heard on every topic is really supporting the group as a whole.

How can you be in **total support** of yourself, the group, and the individuals all at the same time? Our cultural biases are dramatically evident here. Part of being in a progressive, politically-correct culture is that we have an intense focus on and respect for the individual. This is wonderful as long as we also acknowledge that groups have needs as well. Sometimes supporting one individual by letting him/her talk on and on is actively not supporting the group as a whole. Sometimes you simply need to move on.

Micah experienced an excellent example of total support after a Link Crew training program where high school seniors and juniors serve as facilitators for incoming freshmen. Micah asked the upper-class leaders about their experience. One senior said her small group of freshmen started out being very uncooperative and difficult. Micah asked what she did to get through her sessions. She said about halfway through she stopped using the curriculum and just asked the freshmen to tell her what they were looking forward to in high school. The kids were excited to share their ideas with this senior. She listened closely to what they were interested in and then asked if they would like some more information that might help them be successful. At this point she dove back into the curriculum, now with a group that was enthusiastic and interested. Her support of their dreams for high school enabled her to support them with some immediate information they needed. Essentially, she was able to support where they were in the moment while not losing sight of where they needed to be with the curriculum.

There are times when the group process or conversation will not go the way you thought it would or should. Perhaps it has taken a particularly harmful turn and doesn't seem to be a productive conversation any longer. One solution is to breathe into what is happening, step back mentally, and let go. Think **total support**, and see if the conversation shifts. See if you can find the wisdom trying to emerge from the group. Trust it, trust yourself, and trust the group.

You may need to push the group or individuals past their stuck places. Total support means to let everyone's self-worth and participatory ability remain intact while you ask the tough questions. Make the effort to include and, at the same time, move the process and conversation. Keep in mind total support applies to all levels of the group interaction as well as to you. As we grow in our ability to facilitate conversation, we also grow in our ability to hold together the multiple contradictions of total support.

Yes/and, **go big**, and **total support** are mental models for facilitators to keep in mind when working with a group. They should deeply influence the decisions you make as you guide a group to its own wisdom and learning.

Check the Baggage at the Door

To some extent, facilitators cannot avoid bringing their own issues into the process. Notice that nowhere in this book do we claim that a facilitator must be neutral. Although neutrality is certainly a worthy goal in many settings, it is next to impossible. Your life experience, values, beliefs, and habits will intercede despite your best efforts. It is important, however, for the facilitator to have a clear and present mind-set because his/her level of distraction will impact the group and the group process.

Facilitation must incorporate the best of what you have to offer. Your power and passion, your potential must be available to your group as you guide them toward understanding. The real challenge is to bring only those pieces of you that move the group forward. Leave your negative attitudes, distractions, and prejudices behind. We call this process "getting clear." There are many ways to get clear, the following is one example.

Getting Clear (allow 3 to 5 minutes): Breathe in and out slowly. As you do so, notice every part of your body. Move your awareness from your toes to your head. Be sure to give extra attention to your **gut** (for following your intuition), your **hands** (for guiding the group), and your **heart** (for sensing what has heart and meaning). As you breathe in, imagine yourself alive and full and ready for anything. As you exhale, let go and relax into trust and support. Let go of all distractions. Feel energy and focus from every part of your being. Smile inside and outside.

In the End, It's About Being Open to Outcome

Recently, we watched an otherwise talented facilitator throw away a great reflective opportunity. The facilitator was set on having the group notice how they had broken the rules established in the setup to the activity. He was so blinded by this prejudice for learning within the activity he completely missed several participants who wanted to talk about other aspects of the experience. After presenting an

initiative so many times, a facilitator may have a precon-
ceived expectation of what participants should learn. The
challenge is to adapt the "beginner's mind" referred to in
Zen Buddhist philosophy. Each time, try to experience and
debrief an activity with the fresh enthusiasm of the first time
you played and processed.

No matter how valuable, how real, or how useful in life
a set of learning might be, if the participants don't arrive at
the understanding in their own fashion, it is unlikely the
learning will stick. The intention of experiential learning is
to connect participants to their own source of learning and
knowing. The answers are no more in you as a facilitator
than they are in a book or lecture. For the group, the answers
must come from within.

Chapter Three | The 5 Questions

"If you're lucky, you won't find what you're looking for."
—Varekai, Cirque du Soliel

What Are They?

The 5 Questions embody a specific framework for reflective on an experience. They are a collective set of questions for facilitators, beginners as well as seasoned, to use as guideposts in processing an experience with their group. The 5 Questions are a "user-friendly" approach based on the learning cycle as defined by Kolb and Pfeiffer and Jones and discussed in chapter one.

Let's also say a few words about what The 5 Questions are not. They are not a comprehensive learning framework. They do not work every time with every group in every situation. They are a starting place and are not an ending place. For beginning facilitators, we created The 5 Questions to be an easy and practical starting place for reflective conversations. Once you know and have tried The 5 Questions, you can explore deeper and richer learning constructs such as those mentioned in chapter one of this book and in our

Additional Resources section. For experienced facilitators, The 5 Questions becomes a framework from which to ask further questions as you guide participants through the learning cycle.

The 5 Questions have proven to be useful and adaptable to a variety of settings. We have taught them to 14-year-olds who have been able to successfully use them with their peers. Teachers with more than 30 years of experience in the classroom have found them to be valuable tools to add to their repertoire. Experienced facilitators have found worth in both the simple approach and the insight into the study of asking questions. In turn, we benefit from the feedback of these practitioners. They have helped broaden our perspective and expand how we think about and use The 5 Questions.

The 5 Questions

1. Did you notice … ?
2. Why did that happen?
3. Does that happen in life?
4. Who? What? Where? When? Why?
5. What will you do now?

   The questions correlate to most learning cycle methodologies. We most often associate them to the Pfeiffer and Jones approach as seen in figure 3:1. These questions are not random. They are the result of trial-and-error experimentation over thousands of facilitation experiences. The questions each work together to make specific, very general approaches to facilitating learning.

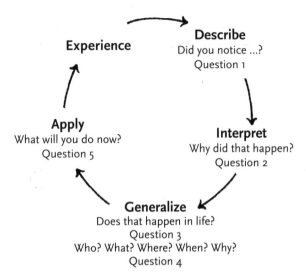

Figure 3:1 The 5 Questions applied to a 5 Stage Learning Cycle model

How Do They Work? Why Do They Work?

Following is an explanation of the purpose of each question in the process, which will give you a more comprehensive view of how and why this model works.

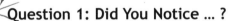

Question 1: Did You Notice ... ?

"Did you notice any fear as you were climbing?"
"Did you notice how hesitant everyone seemed to take the first step?"
"Did you notice anyone taking a leadership role?"
"Did you notice how the protagonist in the novel was set up to fail?"
"Did you notice how the copper reacted to oxygen?"

The question "Did you notice ...?" is an attempt to get participants to look at a specific observation made by the facilitator. The initial reaction of most people after a powerful experience is to want to talk about it. People naturally want to describe what happened to them and how it felt. "Did you notice ...?" allows participants to take part in a conversation about their experience. The facilitator is giving them permission to tell their story.

"Did you notice ... ?" is intentionally not an open-end question and specifically requires a yes/no answer. Many advocate the use of open-end questions to allow participants to describe their experience without bias. We also advocate for open-end questions in most cases, indeed 3 of the 5 questions are open-ended. However, we use this first closed-end question on purpose and with considerable thought. The effect of the entire reflection process can be determined from this seemingly insignificant question. The more a facilitator understands the power of this question, the better the facilitation experience.

Often, the opening question in a reflective discussion does not provide for or create the space for powerful learning. It can, in fact, often be too big a question for the group to tackle first thing after an intensive experiential activity. In the best facilitative environment, participants would be able to discuss their thoughts and feelings around an experience with greater relevancy because they would have total recollection of it. They would be able to identify what they felt, saw, heard, touched, tasted, thought, and smelled. This is often difficult for people to do, however, because we are rarely asked to describe, at any level of detail, something we just experienced. In most learning situations, this process of reflection happens at a subconscious level. When first asking an open-end question such as, "What just happened?" we have found many participants completely unable to describe their experience at any level of useful detail. This is especially true when dealing with young participants (try asking 14-year-olds what they notice sometime) or developmentally challenged participants. When this is the case, the reflection experience is in trouble from the very first question. Here is a possible scenario:

Facilitator: So what did you just experience?
Group: Silence.
Facilitator: Did anyone have any reactions to the experience?
Group: Silence.
Facilitator: Maria, what did you see happen in the group?
Maria: Uh, nothing.
Facilitator: So we just spent 30 minutes, and you guys didn't notice anything?!

Several challenges are potentially at work here. First, it may seem the facilitator has a particular agenda and the group doesn't know that agenda. We are used to teachers having the answers and asking us questions that are "rigged." No one wants to say what s/he experienced for fear of being wrong.

The second challenge could be group members really don't know how to put their experience into words. Certainly they were conscious during it and are likely thinking about certain aspects that affected them, but some find it difficult to put those thoughts into words.

Third, some groups simply don't want to acknowledge they care. Participants are doing their best to pretend they are actually not present. In some groups and/or cultures, answering a question is a sign of emotional commitment that can be easily ridiculed. The rationale is, "If I answer this question, then it means I actually care, and if I care and no one else does, then I look foolish."

The last challenge is that sometimes participants really don't know what just happened, or they do know and feel badly about it, so they don't want to discuss it. Our friend Chellie, a middle-school, assistant principal in Colorado, hears the same thing every parent hears almost every day when calling a student on bad behavior: "Wha'd I do?" The truth is the student is fully aware of what s/he did, but just doesn't want to own it. This can also be true of groups in the reflective process, particularly groups that struggled or exhibited some questionable behavior during the activity. It is difficult for anyone to admit to less than stellar behavior, particularly in front of others.

- We predict scientists will someday uncover the "**Denial Neuron**," the brain cell bandit that sneaks off with particularly incriminating knowledge. Imagine how different corporate scandal hearings might be if there was actually scientific validation supporting a defendant's response of "I cannot recollect that particular piece of information."

Each of these challenges requires a different and potentially nuanced response from a facilitator. The framing of Question 1, "Did you notice ...?" as a closed-end question helps to meet each of these and other challenges head-on.

Question 1 launches us into the **describe/publish/concrete experience stage of learning**. The goal in this stage is to clearly identify what just happened. While many would argue only an open-end question can get a meaningful response, we have found incredible success beginning reflective discussions with this closed-end question.

Starting with a facilitator-driven, **closed-end question** offers at least two distinct advantages. **First**, it allows the facilitator to direct the initial focus of the conversation, thus creating the opportunity to have a somewhat directed conversation. While it is true we advocate remaining open to the outcome of a debriefing, we also believe giving the conversation a guided focus from the outset creates a solid foundation for forthcoming discussion.

The **second** advantage to using a closed-end question is it's easier for participants to answer than an open-end, broader question. This is especially helpful when working with a challenging group. When you ask, "Did you notice ...?" participants can simply nod their heads in response; there really is no risk to them. Once they have nodded their heads, or said yes or no, they have engaged in the observation. More importantly, they have admitted to some level of knowledge. Now you have them. That initial commitment is often all it takes to hook them into a deeper level of reflection.

As you become more skilled as a facilitator, or work with groups that are more capable, it is perfectly fine to begin a group conversation with an open-end question like "What did you notice?" Indeed, for both of us, we use "What did you notice?" or some variation of that question in most of our reflective discussions with adult groups. Ultimately, choosing the type of question to begin reflection comes down to an honest assessment of your facilitative abilities as well as your group's willingness to engage.

So, what do you notice? The first question requires one critical skill: **observation**. Becoming a powerful observer ought to be a facilitator's first task. In every group experience there are literally innumerable issues that might be raised. Take the time to ask yourself what you are observing. Why did that piece of information rise to the top of the million other possibilities?

The **objective of observation** is to provide a mirror for participants to look into and to open up the possibility for learning from what they see. The things you notice as a facilitator guide your understanding and capability to help a group learn. Some things in every group experience are more worthy of notice than others. Observing what a facilitator notices often says more about the facilitator than about the group's experience. As we observe our own observations, we gain the power to look inside the process of facilitation itself. Now that is paying attention!

Imagine a group playing an activity called Team Juggle (see page 106). This initiative requires team members to work together to keep a certain number of objects in the air. For instance, the team might be randomly throwing four tennis balls around the circle with the intent of keeping all the balls moving and not having any one of the team members drop a ball.

As the facilitator, you notice the team never stops the action to discuss possible strategies. They are simply having a great time throwing the balls at each other. Your first question might be, "Did you notice you never stopped the action to discuss strategy?" This will launch the group into a reflection about strategy and planning. If, however, your first question is based on a different observation, the conversation could go in an entirely different direction. For example, "Did you notice John consistently passed to Mario, and Chelsea never got the ball?" This might send the group into a dialogue about skills and abilities as well as fairness and teamwork. Both issues were present at the same time in the group, along with probably twenty other relevant issues. The question becomes, what are you as the facilitator trying to bring to the attention of your group?

The way you approach observation will inform the initial direction and focus of the reflective conversation. Take a moment to consider the different questions you might ask yourself as a facilitator. For instance, you may take a **scientific approach** and look for some of the following data sets:

- How much time elapsed?
- Who contributed and how much?
- Was the objective reached?
- How many different strategies were tried?

By looking for data, you open up a frank conversation about what actually occurred. What can be measured and compared? You can focus the dialogue along the lines of what a group was attempting to achieve versus what was actually achieved.

Using an **anthropological approach** might mean observing by setting yourself up as an outsider, able to see the interaction of the group in ways the group itself cannot. You might expand to a more holistic approach, and ask what you are not seeing that you should:

- Who had power in the group?
- How did they acquire that power?
- Under what rules did the group operate?
- Which rules were followed? Which broken?
- What assumptions were made?

When you look at each group as a mini-society with their own customs and silent protocols, the worlds of culture and habit collide into a fascinating opportunity for new learning.

A third option is to take a **psychological approach**. We do not mean you should attempt to solve individual pathologies but merely take the opportunity to look closely at individuals and their behaviors. The following questions might be appropriate:

- Why did she take a leadership role?
- Was anyone displaying strong emotions?
- How did he react to being consistently ignored?
- _____ seemed frustrated early on. How could you tell?
- Who was most focused on completing the task?

Looking deeply at individuals and then raising possibilities with the group can often provide profound reflection.

As you can see, careful and creative observation is the key to asking the question that can open your group to reflection and focus their attention. Following up with Question 2 leads them further down the path of powerful learning possibilities.

What If They DIDN'T Notice?

What happens when you ask participants if they noticed something, and they look at you blankly and say, "No, we didn't notice that"? Are you done? In a word, no.

Three directions are possible in this case. First, you can help them think through or replay the experience in their mind and see if, upon reflection, they do notice it. Second, you might be able to have them build on your observation with one of their own. Finally, you may have to simply abandon that observation and start over with another one.

As we learned in chapter one, the brain is taking in way more data than it is capable of processing. A great deal of what is happening around us at any given moment is missed. The incredible thing about the brain, however, is that often things just outside the periphery of our attention can easily be brought into our attention with a simple request. In fact, we can experiment right now. Look up from this book and pay attention to a sound in your environment right now that you were unaware of until we just asked you to notice it. Got one? Probably it happened immediately. You might have been able to notice a sound as soon as you read the word sound! By simply calling attention to a sense or experience, our brain automatically makes it more relevant for us.

As a facilitator, we can use this technique to **replay the experience** and open groups to notice things they might otherwise miss. The conversation may go like this:

Facilitator: Did you notice no one asked the goal of the exercise?
Group: No. We didn't notice.
Facilitator: Well think back for a second. In the entire experience, did anyone ask for the goal?

Group: Ummmmm, I guess not.

The second approach is to **have groups come up with their own observation**. Because the act of saying, "No, we didn't notice that" is also a commitment to comment at all, it will often open groups for further comments. In which case, the conversation might sound like this:

Facilitator: Did you notice no one asked the goal of the exercise?

Group: No.

Facilitator: Well, what do you remember asking about?

Group: Well, we asked a lot about the rules, like how much time we had and whether we could use any additional materials.

Sometimes, we facilitators must admit temporary defeat and **redirect**. Some groups simply are not aware of what just happened, and maybe don't want to be. Remember, we cannot learn from something we did not notice. Forcing groups to notice or highlighting ignorance will produce only frustration for you and the group. Therefore, you might need to redirect:

Facilitator: Did you notice no one asked the goal of the exercise?

Group: No, there was no purpose.

Facilitator: Think back, did anyone ask about the goal of the exercise?

Group: Who cares?

Facilitator: Do you notice that no one seems engaged in talking about this right now? (redirected Did you notice...?)

Group: Obviously.

Question 2: Why Did That Happen?

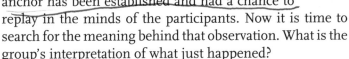

At this point in the reflective process, you have hopefully gained some ground with your group. With either a yes answer or a nod of the head, your group has admitted to noticing something about the activity you just experienced. An observational anchor has been established and had a chance to replay in the minds of the participants. Now it is time to search for the meaning behind that observation. What is the group's interpretation of what just happened?

Question 2 is associated with the **interpretation stage of learning**. A great number of learning cycle models leave this stage out entirely—in part, because many adult groups interpret on their own, moving swiftly from describing their actions ("We worked well together") to interpreting their actions ("We worked so well together because we have really gotten to know each other"). Although many people do this on their own, it is important for the facilitator to be able to keep track of whether individuals actually have interpreted and at what level. Sometimes facilitators want to skip quickly past asking for the group's interpretation of the activity and go directly to asking what the grouped learned and having them make other connections. That will only be successful if the group really understands the motivation, causation, or meaning behind the actions or feelings they experienced.

Humans have searched for meaning longer than recorded history. As a species, it seems we are not content to just observe things. We search for explanations and then create our own interpretations for why things happen. This natural desire is to our advantage as facilitators. No matter how challenging the group, participants can barely resist trying to find meaning once they have committed to an observation. The more powerful and interesting the observation, the more hooked participants will be in the search for why it happened. A typical exchange might go as follows:

Facilitator: Did you notice how long it took the group to develop a solution? (Question 1)

Participant: Yes, it took a long time, and it was really frustrating!

Facilitator: Why did that happen? (Question 2)

Participant: Well, we didn't understand the rules at first, and no one asked for clarification, so we wasted a lot of time on ideas that weren't possible.

As an alternative to reframing when a group doesn't notice an observation as discussed earlier, this question can work well whether the group did or did not notice the issue raised by the facilitator. The question just changes slightly from "Why did that happen?" to, "Why did you not notice?" The objective is simply to help participants move from the stage of reliving their experience through describing their actions and feelings, to one of interpreting those actions and feelings.

As participants struggle to make sense of their actions, behaviors, and feelings, there is one important pitfall to watch for: a lack of information, causing an **inaccurate interpretation.** Take a look at any population of adolescent children. They are continually struggling to make sense of the observations they are making and sometimes come up with amazing and all-encompassing rationalizations: "She doesn't like me because I don't have the right jeans!" "If you don't step on a crack, nothing bad will happen" (at least hopefully your mother's back will be safe—knock on wood). "I got a bad grade because the teacher doesn't like me." The list can go on and on.

We, as adults, are also not immune to inaccurate interpretation. Consider the difficulty we often have in accepting responsibility for a mistake we have made. How easy is it to blame someone else? What about a friend who acts rudely to you one day? It's easy to immediately consider the person may not like you anymore when the case may be the person simply had just received some bad news and was not in the mood to talk. On a more global scale, every day we can observe the personal conflict and societal discontent inspired by varied interpretations of either political or religious beliefs.

It is the accuracy with which we interpret that determines what we learn from any given event in our lives. This is true with reflective activities as well. What do you do when the answers are not entirely accurate—either way off base or slightly skewed? How do you help participants come to the realization that other interpretations could be more accurate and could take them to a deeper level of learning? This is when you take the group to the next step and dig a little deeper, using a form of Question 2.

Why did that *really* happen? Two things are required to help your groups connect their observations to accurate interpretation. **First**, you must make sure you made a careful and accurate observation. When you ask, "Did you notice ...?" make sure the group is really all on the same page with the observation. In other words, whether the response is yes or no, there has to be a commitment that they either did observe what you noticed, or they did not observe it. Either answer is fine, but the commitment to observation is key.

Second, when you ask "Why did that happen?" listen closely. You are not listening for a "right answer;" you are listening for an answer that is accurate and connected. *↳ to what did you notice!*

Let's review a potential conversation:

Facilitator: Did you notice I was able to win every game? (Question 1)

Participant: Yes. How did you do that?

Facilitator: What do you think? Why did I win each time? (Question 2)

Participant: You cheated!

Facilitator: Well, cheating means I played by different rules. I played by the same rules you did each time, didn't I? If I didn't cheat, why did I **really** win each time? (Question 2—restated)

Participant: You played before, you know the strategy.

Facilitator: So you think I was able to win because I knew the strategy? (Reflection)

Participant: Yes.

The facilitator began by highlighting the observation that she was able to win each time. Once the participants were anchored in the acknowledgment of the observation, the facilitator moved on to Question 2, "Why did that happen?" The immediate response was not an accurate interpretation of the reason why the facilitator won (we are talking about an extremely honest facilitator here); rather it was completely unsupported and false. So instead of moving on to the third question, the facilitator acknowledged the initial comment but did not let participants stop there. She continued on, asking the same question, just in a different way. By pressing participants to really examine and understand why a particular behavior occurred, the facilitator enabled the group to learn relevant, accurate information as a result of the experience.

Consider another scenario in which participants are reluctant to own their behavior:

> Facilitator: Did you notice that each person went down the same path and came to the same dead end? (Question 1)
> Participant: Yes.
> Facilitator: Why did that happen? (Question 2)
> Participant: Because the path is confusing.
> Facilitator: **Yes, and** what else might have caused everyone to make the same mistake? (Question 2—restated)
> Participant: Well, maybe they were scared the rest of the group would be mad at them if they took a step in a different direction.

In this example, the participant wanted to blame the hesitation on the path rather than the participants. Often participants look for a scapegoat in the activity itself rather than taking a risk and identifying themselves as culpable. The reality that every participant followed the same dead-end path is clear but does not really get to the heart of what else may have been going on with this activity. In this case, the facilitator simply acknowledged and then probed for additional explanations by asking another form of the question "Why did that happen?" The resulting conversation ought to lead to a more accurate and clear interpretation of the meaning behind the activity, such as how dangerous it is to blindly follow the masses or how important it is to think for yourself. As facilitators, we want to encourage participation, help the discovery of accurate interpretation, and also help the group look more deeply at causation.

Restating Question 2 with the implication you are asking "Why did this **really** happen?" will help uncover more learning for the group. It is important to understand that asking a group to probe deeper into the whys of an event can be powerful and therefore dangerous territory, especially if the group appears reluctant. Deciding to "push" a group or individual, inviting them to a deeper level, is a judgment call on the part of the facilitator. Rely on intuition and experience to discern if the group has gotten to the heart of a particular moment.

A word of caution. Even the most experienced facilitators can be wrong. Allow yourself the confidence to press a group to really understand why a given behavior or feeling occurred, but also accept the humility of being wrong and moving on if the group is not seeing what you are seeing.

Once grounded in a working interpretation, the group is ready for Question 3.

Question 3: Does It Happen in Life?

With the first two questions, we focus only on the specific experience, nothing else. It's the third question that invites participants to generalize the experience, asking them to look at it in broader terms and see if there is any connection between the specific experience they just had and what happens in their lives. If participants are only asked to think about and discuss the proximate experience, they have no opportunity to transfer any understanding or learning from the current experience. The facilitator's job is to help the group uncover those connections by asking participants to consider how the activity could be relevant to them.

Trying to help participants generalize their learning from a specific experience and acknowledge there may be similarities in behavior elsewhere in their lives is something we have come to refer to as **"climbing over the wall of learning."** People who climb over the wall of learning are able to see the connection between an observation in an initial experience to a situation in the future. People who don't make it over the wall of learning are doomed to repeat the same lesson over and over again in a variety of different contexts.

While it is not difficult to learn a specific lesson, it is often a challenge for one to see how that single lesson matters in other areas of life. For instance, our brain immediately records the painful, specific lesson of touching a hot pot on a stove and getting burned, making it unlikely we will touch the same pot on the same stove twice. The real challenge comes in using the experience of touching the hot pot and the observation that it hurts to avoid touching other hot things regardless of shape, size, and material in the future.

Many times in reflecting, a group will be able to easily identify what happened in the activity and may even be able to understand why it happened. However, it is not always easy for groups to make the connections between a simulated activity and real life events. It can be very difficult for a group to see that similar behaviors can happen in many different contexts and the learning from one experience can possibly be generalized to others. Many discussion models rely upon simple phrasing to create the generalization, like, "So What" or "What do you learn from this?" Although direct and sometimes effective, we have seen many previously talkative groups go dead silent when this question is thrown out. Sometimes it is simply too broad or too intimidating to answer. Or perhaps it was asked at the wrong time in the reflection process.

Another impediment to a successful group conversation happens when a facilitator jumps in to rescue a group struggling to find the answers and provides the "appropriate learning." Although this is extremely tempting, we encourage you not to do it. Giving away the answer might make you feel better and more accomplished, and some group members might even grasp what you are saying. The facilitator's job, however, is not to process for the group but to invite participants to make the connections that lead them to find their own answers. Fight the temptation to "know" and instead work to become curious about what the group knows. How will participants answer the difficult questions about how the feelings and behaviors they experienced connect to other parts of their lives? By encouraging them to struggle, you open up greater opportunities for long-lasting learning.

Within The 5 Questions approach, Question 3 is another closed-end question used to guide participants to the next level. This is a specific and highly effective technique to help participants climb over the wall of learning and generalize their observations. As simple as it sounds, asking "Does it happen in life?" allows participants to more easily connect the observation from the activity to similar observations made in other parts of their lives. Consider the following conversation:

> Facilitator: Did you notice how vocal and loud John was at the beginning of the exercise? (Question 1)
> Participant: Yes. He quickly became the leader.
> Facilitator: Why did that happen? (Question 2)
> Participant: He was the loudest, so we just started listening to what he said.
> Facilitator: Does that happen in life? Does the loudest person sometimes become the leader? (Question 3)
> Participant: Yes, that is often true. The loudest person can sway others toward his or her point of view, even when I know everyone disagrees.

Having anchored firmly in the experience as well as the specific observation from that experience, the facilitator is able to ask the group to reflect further. Ideally, Question 3 is phrased in such a way participants can easily relate it to their own experience. If you are working with students, you might change the question to, "Does that happen at school?" If you are working in a corporate setting, you may ask, "Does that happen at work?" Bringing a specific context to mind allows participants to clearly connect the observation to their real-life experience and previous observations.

This phase of questioning opens up the **abstract conceptualization phase of learning**. At this point, the task is to bring the participants out of the specific experience and into an observation of the patterns at work in themselves or with others. Without focused facilitation, participants may stay mired in their direct experience or may translate only the emotionally charged aspects of an experience, thus never being able to get over the wall of learning. You can see this happening when participants seem to want to talk endlessly about the experience they just had.

The following two scenarios could be the result of a highly emotionally-charged experience where one member of the group is feeling hurt and slighted. Left to her own devices, it would be easy to imagine her reflecting in the following way:

> Facilitator: Did you notice you were frustrated during this experience? (Question 1)
> Participant: Yes, I hated it.
> Facilitator: Why did you hate it? (Question 2)
> Participant: Because these people are jerks. I wish I had never done this. I am not going to do this kind of experience again.
> Facilitator: How come? (Asking for explanation)
> Participant: Because it was so uncomfortable.
> Facilitator: What made you uncomfortable? (Question 2 again)
> Participant: Oh, I don't know. Maybe how rude people were or how they didn't want to help and ... I don't know; it was just terrible.

The participant correctly identified a powerful emotion, hate, then took only the briefest moment to reflect on the source of this emotion: "These people are jerks." That may be an accurate assessment based on her observation and judgment. Left to a facilitator who continues to focus on only the present moment, there really will be no opportunity for generalized learning to occur. Rather than having an opportunity to think about the way in which this experience could mirror her experience in other contexts, she simply shuts down, having learned only one thing—she will never again put herself into this kind of specific situation. In this scenario, the participant is stuck on one side of the wall of learning, staying only in her interpretation of the experience and avoiding any connection to life beyond the experience. She will most likely not be able to get over the wall of learning without help. Without the right questions, this participant will not see patterns or connections between this situation and other situations in her life. Therefore all opportunity for powerful, relevant, and meaningful learning is lost.

For the facilitator to help make the connection, the conversation might be something like the following:

Facilitator: Did you notice you were frustrated during this experience? (Question 1)

Participant: Yes, I hated it.

Facilitator: Why did you hate it? (Question 2)

Participant: Because these people are jerks. I wish I had never done this. I am not going to do this kind of experience again.

Facilitator: Does that happen to you sometimes at work? Do you have to work with people you don't like or do an assignment you don't like to do? (Question 3)

Participant: Yeah, sometimes you have to work with people you don't get along with and do things you don't think are fun.

Rather than focusing exclusively on what a miserable time she is having in the immediate situation and what jerks these people are, she is now thinking about the fact that similar observations can be made in other contexts. She is climbing over the wall of learning and now open to a variety of possible connections. She may choose to look at why she doesn't get along with people or the specific triggers that set her bad feelings in motion. She may, alternatively, look more closely at how she might deal with people she doesn't like in more productive ways. Hopefully, she will find meaning and a sense of empowerment as she learns more about herself and others. With proper reflection, the experience still holds out the opportunity for a generalized and useful connection.

Often groups and/or individuals have difficulty identifying and accepting aspects of their own behavior. A facilitator can be especially helpful in guiding the group to recognize and discuss those blind spots. That is exactly the power of an experiential simulation or activity. A facilitator helps by asking the hard question, "Does that happen in life as well?" Although participants may struggle with the answer, this question can begin the group on a rewarding journey.

- **What if it doesn't?** Everyone once and awhile we are asked what to do when someone says "No, it doesn't happen in life." Put bluntly, this is always a lie. The patterns that show up during an exercise are micro patterns of daily life. The answer really is, "Yes, this happens in life." On those rare occasions when someone really doesn't want to admit to a connection, it simply takes a gentle reframing of the question or a reminder of the behavior: "So you are saying you are not typically loud in real life?" or "Wait, let me ask that again. Do groups sometimes rush into action without asking for clarification on the rules or boundaries?"

  Generally, with just a little gentle prodding, participants begin to see the action, behaviors, and feelings present during their experience are also present in dozens of places in their life. Your job as a facilitator is to help them make that connection clear.

Question 4: Who? What? Where? When? Why?—The Anchor Stage

The Anchor Stage is specifically relevant for working with student groups, but it's important to understand for adult groups as well. Once you have a commitment to transfer the learning from Question 3, anchor that transfer in a real world experience that reflects the same behavior or pattern. Although tricky to describe, this is really a natural process for most people and groups. In fact, the reason we don't emphasize this question as much for adult groups is because many groups do this automatically. You often hear a conversation like this:

> Facilitator: Does that happen in life? (Question 3)
> Participant: Yeah, it definitely does. I was just saying to a friend the other day that I need to stop listening to the loudest voices in my life and start listening to the wisest. My Dad is naturally loud, and he gets a lot of attention because of it. I think I have just learned to follow loud people as a result of growing up with him.

In this case, the participant, answered not just the question asked, which is really just a yes or no question, but went on to fill in the obvious next step—where in life do you see this behavior or pattern.

Question 4, therefore, can be any version of the traditional "5 Ws" (Who, What, Where, When, Why) that anchor the group in a real life example of the observation and interpretation made in Questions 1 and 2. Examples might include:

> Where do you see that in your life?
> Who do you know that behaves that way?

When have you seen that same thing occur?
What do you mean when you say you see that operating
in your life?
Why do you think people do that in general?

The function of this question is similar to that of Question
2. It exists to follow up on the commitment made in response
to Question 3. Participants acknowledge they either do or do
not see a connection between the specific experience and their
everyday lives. Question 4 helps them tease out the patterns
and causal relationships underlying that connection.

Facilitator: Did you notice how successful you were on
the third try? (Question 1)
Participant: Yes, that was awesome!
Facilitator: Why did that happen? (Question 2)
Participant: We stopped fighting about the "right" way
and decided to just start trying ideas. That really helped
because we immediately started working together.
Facilitator: Does that happen in life? (Question 3)
Participant: Sure, sometimes.
Facilitator: Where have you seen that? (Question 4)
Participant: Well, sometimes you need to stop talking
about how to do stuff and just try it. At work we have a
motto to "fail forward fast." Just last week we decided to
just get a prototype built and not worry whether or not
it met every specification. By not wasting energy fighting, we have more energy to put into moving forward.

Notice how, in this example, the answer to Question 4
sounds very similar to the answer to Question 2, with the
exception that it is no longer about the specific experience
the participants just had. In this stage, they should be talk-

ing about their lives beyond the current experience. This is exactly as it should be and is one indication the participant is climbing over the wall of learning.

Give me an example. We often find that rather than asking a question, it can be just as profound to simply ask the group to give you an example. Phrases like:

"Give me an example."
"Tell me about a time when that was true."
"For instance...."

These phrases simply extend the invitation for participants to go further down the road they are already walking when they admit, "Yes, this does happen in life." With just a little prodding, most groups love to make the connection between the specific actions or feelings in an experience and those same actions or feelings in other areas of life. It can even lead to some amazing "aha" moments as participants start to see connections they missed before.

Micah was facilitating a leader training in Napa, CA, and noticed the boys were much more active and vocal than the girls. The conversation went something like this:

Micah: Did you notice the boys were much more active and involved in this exercise than the girls? (Question 1)
Participant: Yes.
Micah: Why do you think that was true? (Questions 2)
Female Participant: (after much thought and an extended period of silence) Well, I think the boys just felt kind of entitled to be involved, and because they were so vocal, I didn't really have a chance to talk.
Micah: Does that happen in life? (Question 3)
Participants: (heads nodding, no one saying anything)

Micah: Well, can someone give me an example of where boys are vocal in life and sometimes girls don't feel like they have a chance to speak up?

Female Participant: (again after an extended silence) Well, to be honest, everywhere. This is a pretty sexist school in a lot of ways, and boys just kind of feel like they can get away with anything. In student government recently, we were talking about a theme for the year, and a few of the louder boys just shouted everyone else down until they got their way.

Once a pattern is identified, it almost becomes a game to see how that pattern is playing itself out. You can even do this with yourself. Micah recently had this internal conversation:

Micah: Did you notice you misplaced your keys again?

Self: Yes.

Micah: Why did that happen?

Self: Well, when I came in last, I was in a hurry and didn't put the keys in the spot where I generally put them.

Micah: Does this happen a lot in life? Is this a pattern?

Self: Unfortunately, yes!

Micah: Where? Give me some examples.

Self: Well, last week when I came back from a run. The other day when I came home with the kids. Pretty much anytime I feel rushed right as I walk in the door.

By having the "self-talk" moment, it becomes blazingly clear where a blind spot might be. Once you shed a little light on the pattern, correcting it seems almost self-evident.

Question 5: What Will You Do Now?

Finally, this is the heart of the model. Fundamentally, the final question of any experiential exercise is "How will you be different in the future as a result of this experience?" It is important for participants to face this question head on and recognize the responsibility of using their newly acquired information. What is the difference between having information and not using it, and not having the information at all? The experience will have been useless unless it creates some impetus to modify behavior in the future. At this point in the process, participants often meet and must scale the second wall of learning.

The Wall of Learning (Take 2)

How many times have you made the same mistake twice? We are guessing more than once. Our brains are not well equipped to learn from every single experience. We learn from those things that make it all the way through the cycle. This last stop on the cycle of learning—**applying** the knowledge to future action—is the most important and often most difficult. Our mind puts up a huge wall for a couple of important reasons.

One reason why participants hit this second wall of learning is **fear**. Publicly stating their future intentions begins the process of making them accountable for change. Knowing it will require some changes on their part causes participants to anticipate the discomfort and anxiety that could be involved. As a facilitator, your objective is simply to provide a safe and supportive environment in which to make those declarations. State the question boldly and encourage participants to take it seriously.

Another reason participants hit this second wall of learning is **ambiguity**. If they have not really understood the connection between their experience and the way they operate in the world, they cannot clearly state their intention to use that information. This requires the facilitator to back up and re-ask Questions 3 and 4. Encourage participants to really think about the connections and to draw conclusions meaningful to them in their experience.

For a learning to first transfer to long-term memory, and then be strong enough to change future behavior, requires the brain's synaptic connections literally be changed. This can happen in a number of ways.

Repetition plays a major role in learning. Simply rehashing the same point in multiple ways and asking participants to continue to reflect on what they would do differently can create change. Sometimes we do not have the luxury of time and repetition, lest our participants get bored and we lose focus in the moment.

Emotion and intention are also significant contributors to learning. Getting participants to change their behavior in the future means associating the change as emotionally positive in some way—at a basic level, either pleasure-enhancing or pain-reducing. The opportunity for real change is further enhanced with stated intention. A shift occurs when a participant makes a bold statement such as, "Next time, I will check to make sure everyone has been heard. If I do that, then we can avoid some of the hurt feelings we had in this experience." Making this statement reinforces the learning and connects it to a future state where pleasure is enhanced and/or pain is reduced.

Where? To help participants take a declaration to the next level, we often ask the follow-up question, **"Where specifically will that be useful?"** This is a way of visualizing that future. We liken it to goal-setting: The more specific you make the goal, the more clearly you see it, and the more likely you are to achieve it.

Some participants may feel it is redundant or intrusive to be pushed into making context-specific declarations. The following conversation can create some discomfort:

> Facilitator: Why does that happen? (Question 4)
> Participant: Because people are sometimes afraid to make a mistake. If you think people will judge you, then it is hard to decide when you know it might be wrong. I know it is not always the best thing, but that is what people do.
> Facilitator: Give me an example. (Question 4)
> Participant: I don't know. I guess I often hold back with my friends because I don't want to say the wrong thing and look foolish.
> Facilitator: What will you do now? (Question 5)
> Participant: Well, I try to just not care what people think. I make the best decision I can and try to move forward.
> Facilitator: Where specifically will that be useful? (Question 5 – where?)
> Participant: Umm. I guess I am thinking a lot about college right now. Everyone is giving me advice, but I don't think anybody really knows. I want to listen to everyone, but ultimately, it has to be my decision.

As the participant struggles to think about where the specific lesson would be useful, his/her mind begins to cycle through possibilities. It can often stop in places where eminent and difficult decisions need to be made, or exacting changes need to occur. Committing to a course of action in these places can be challenging, even overwhelming. We can sometimes help participants by asking them if they think the lesson they learned or the connection they made was a good one. Recalling whether they liked the direction of the reflection process to that point can solidify and reinforce the courage necessary to declare a future course of action.

Whether participants learn from experience to the point of changing their ways can only be known by them. Our opportunity with "What will you do now?" is to help them fast-forward briefly and set down a path that might make change possible.

The 5 Questions—Working Together

The 5 Questions reveal a cycle, and in rare circumstances, a group will actually follow the circular path. We have indeed experienced reflective moments as simple as the following:

Facilitator: Did you notice that I won every game?
Participant: Yes.
Facilitator: Why did that happen?
Participant: Because you have played it before. You know the strategy! If you know the strategy, it is easy to win.
Facilitator: Does that happen in school?
Participant: Of course!
Facilitator: Why does that happen? Give me an example.

Participant: Well, the person who knows the strategy has an advantage over the person who doesn't. I mean, just doing my homework everyday first thing when I get home is a strategy. When I do, I know I do better in school.

Facilitator: What will you do now that you know that?

Participant: Well, I suppose I should look for other places where strategies would be helpful. I want to become a better soccer player, and I could probably find some strategies to do that.

This kind of conversation is rare. An innumerable amount of challenges arise in the course of a single debrief. People backtrack and repeat themselves. People are at different places in processing the information. Groups fail to make even obvious connections. They get stuck on particular ideas and themes.

The reflection process challenges everyone. Like any skill, the more you practice it and pay attention to yourself, the better you get. If your practice involves giving away the answers, talking more than the group, or skipping questions, you will only make yourself better at unsuccessful methods.

With time, patience, and coaching, reflection can become one of the more powerful tools in your educational tool kit. It has the power to transform and enlighten. At its best, it takes the facilitator off the stage and puts each participant in touch with his or her own center of knowledge and power.

Why 5? Why Not 4? Why Not 17?

We like the structure of five questions with the pattern of questioning following a closed, open, closed, open, open structure for a variety of reasons. The first is **practical**. As we attempted to teach both more and less complicated structures, they were often either not comprehensive enough or too comprehensive to be of practical value to new facilitators.

The second is more **theoretical**. The five questions connect explicitly to each of the stages in the learning cycle in very conscious ways. We move deliberately and smoothly through observation, causation/interpretation, generalization, and application. This allows for a deliberate and open style of facilitation, which has generated enormously productive conversations for us and the groups with which we work.

Different trainers, researchers, and teachers have used different sets of questions to touch the same essential stops. Our objective here is to lay out one approach that we have found extremely useful across a wide variety of participants. Let us remind you that our approach is a road map and not a definitive, inflexible guide. The intention is to use The 5 Questions as a tool set that can guide a facilitative process. The more you use them and focus on the reflective experience, the more skilled you will become in knowing when to alter or embellish them.

Chapter Four

Keep the Conversation Moving

"But this bridge will only take you halfway there—
the last few steps you'll have to take alone."
—Shel Silverstein

You know The 5 Questions, you start asking them, and
you get some good answers. Then a silence falls over the
group, or you notice several people have tuned out. Sometimes participants want to contribute more or less information than is appropriate, or they want to communicate in a
different way than the group requires. A variety of obstacles
can prevent a group from moving forward.

No matter how perfectly you set up an experience. No
matter how smoothly the experience itself goes. When you
start to reflect or talk about what just happened, all kinds
of things pop up to make a fruitful conversation difficult.
When this happens, some level of tension is created. What
do you do? The ability to effectively resolve that tension can
be the difference between a good facilitator and a great one.
This chapter is focused on sharing some of the techniques
that have worked well for us.

Conflict and Resistance

Let's just put it out there. Conflict exists. People will disagree. They will get heated and emotional. It's okay. In fact, we know from studying group development the most healthy and productive groups have conflicts and, through experience, figure out how to work through them. As a facilitator, you must learn to embrace conflict and work with it. It won't help you or the group if your strategy is to avoid conflict. Go ahead; jump in.

Resistance, a form of conflict, will also emerge. For a variety of reasons, participants will be reluctant to participate. Your job as the facilitator is to determine how much to invite resistant group members into the conversation, and how much to let them be. It is trial and error and requires you to hone the skill of reading people in any given moment. That's the art of facilitation. Following are some tools and strategies that will help you deal with both resistance and conflict in your groups.

"Tell Me More"

This is our all-time-favorite thing to say to encourage people to talk. We might even argue they are three of the most powerful words you can use in relationships. Quiet or reluctant group members often need a bit of extra encouragement to elaborate on their thoughts and observations. Many participants contribute only the bare minimum unless invited to share more.

- Curiously, it doesn't usually take much encouragement to get a person talking. Just a simple **"Tell me more"** can do the trick.
- This request must be made with absolute, genuine curiosity

and authenticity. It has to be real. If you don't actually want the person to tell you more and you stop listening midway through the telling, group members take note and begin to shut down. Therefore, choose wisely when you ask to be told more. Make sure you and the group are prepared to listen.

When conducting workshops with parents, the topic of the ritual, after-school question will come up: "What did you do in school today?" The typical response is "Nothing" or a variation thereof. Our consistent advice to parents is to smile, lean forward, look their child in the eyes, and say, "Wow, tell me more." Clearly, there shouldn't be more to say about "nothing." However time and again, parents are amazed by how much more their children have to say about "nothing."

We have discovered many people are conditioned to believe others don't really care about their opinion. Being marginalized and not really listened to is a daily experience for many of us. Naturally, it follows that in a group experience, people may not expect others to be interested in their comments. An honest, "Tell me more" goes a long way toward convincing people that you are serious about wanting to hear what they have to say. The best encouragement participants can have is an appreciative, curious audience. It's fun to see people open up and relax into being heard.

Variations of "Tell me more"

- Please say more about that.
- What does that look/feel like?
- Tell us more about that.
- Go on.
- Okay, and then what?

Silence

Silence is complex and inevitable. A skilled facilitator must be able to discern what the silence is about and respond appropriately. Often, in the quiet moments, creative solutions can emerge—becoming comfortable with the silence that is part of the rhythm of group processing is important.

There are processing models dealing almost entirely with silence. Journaling, reflective walks, silent meditation, and others have a significant place in the realm of reflection techniques. For our purposes, however, we are assuming the silence is something we don't want to sustain. We want somehow to bring our group back into conversation. How do we do that?

Silence can indicate the facilitator may have asked an off-track or unclear question. You need to trust your intuition and learn to read your group in order to determine what the situation is and how best to respond. Figure 4:1 represents some options we use when faced with silence.

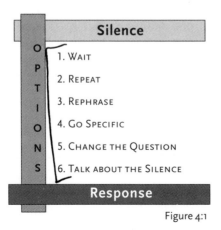

Silence

OPTIONS

1. Wait
2. Repeat
3. Rephrase
4. Go Specific
5. Change the Question
6. Talk about the Silence

Response

Figure 4:1

1. Wait: Let there be silence.

Count to seven in your head to give them "think time." This will work when the silence exists because people are truly thinking. What an amazing feeling to be thinking so hard about a question you are not aware of what others are doing. Thinking deeply about a question is an opportunity for deeper reflection. If you reach seven in your head, and no one has said anything, it might be time to move to the next strategy.

Occasionally, we will actually manufacture silence. This can be especially important when a few participants are dominating the conversation. Let the group know you are going to ask a question, and you are not going to take immediate answers. After asking the question, slowly count to seven in your head, and then see if a few different people are ready to participate.

2. Repeat: Ask the question again.

If you are confident your question has relevance for the group, then simply restate it. Saying it again can spark all kinds of new reflection in the group. On occasion, we have noticed a silence so deep the group was just reluctant to break it. By restating the question, you break the silence and once again give the group permission to respond. If they don't respond quickly this time, it is time to move on. Do not wait for seven seconds a second time. That is a sure way to turn a powerful, reflective silence into an awkward, oppressive silence.

3. Rephrase: Ask the question in a slightly different way.

You asked the group, "Why did that happen?" and got no response. Try rephrasing the question to make it more accessible: "So you noticed no one took a leadership role;

why do you think no one stepped into that role?" By simply altering the way you asked the question, you could help the group think about it in a different way.

Remember The 5 Questions are merely guideposts and not formulaic steps. Change your language while maintaining the intent of the question in order to approach the group differently. As in the previous example, it often helps to wrap a summary of the conversation so far into the question to help the group stay present with the thought process.

If you are still getting nowhere, it is time for more dramatic action.

4. Go specific.

Ask a group member by name to answer the question. This is where the facilitator starts putting some skin in the game. By this point, the group has noticed the silence. Calling on a specific person will both remove the pressure from the group and place a lot more pressure on one single participant. Our experience suggests you need to choose this person with some care. Look for the person who seems on the verge of sharing but just needs a little push. When one person has spoken, it may help break the barrier for others. If the person you asked has a difficult time responding, then it is time to change your strategy. At some point, we must acknowledge the problem may not be in the group.

5. Change the question.

Assume it was a bad question. Go in a different direction. For example, imagine a teacher who shows a civil war video to her class. The video contains numerous themes as well as visual and statistical data. It may provoke all kinds of reactions within the class. When the lights come on, the teacher strides to the middle of the class and asks, "So, what did you learn from that?" She is amazed when the class is starkly silent. The problem here may not be that the students are not thinking; indeed they are likely processing a lot inside their minds. The problem could be she has asked a question about generalized learning while the class is still thinking about what it was they just saw. They still need to publish and describe their experience. By changing the question to "Did you notice ..." or "What did you see in the video?" the teacher is more likely to receive a response.

6. Name the silence and talk about the silence.

"It's really quiet in here; what's going on?" Sometimes it turns out the experience to be reflected upon is the reflection process itself. We have some of our most powerful moments as facilitators when we simply call the group out and name the behavior. Being a diligent observer should not end when the experience is over because truly the experience and the reflection process are not separate. What learning is available to the group when you name the silence?

What If You Did Know? Take a Guess

The most common teenage response to virtually any question is "I don't know." We are constantly amazed by how little 15-year-olds seem to know when asked a question. Funny, because most often, they do know. In reality, they are afraid of looking stupid, not saying the right thing, or being vulnerable in front of others. There is great fear in owning the knowledge they have, particularly in front of others.

"What if you did know?" is, more often than not, exactly the right thing to ask, and sure enough, with very little pause, you get a response. Here's an example:

Facilitator: Why do you think most people sit in the same place every day at lunch?

Participant: I don't know.

Facilitator: What if you did know?

Participant: Well, I don't know, I guess people maybe don't want to try new things. And, you know, once you get comfortable with one group, you don't really want to try anything else. I mean, what if the new group doesn't like you?

The participant was reluctant to own the knowledge and opinion he had about people and their behavior. As the facilitator, the challenge is to listen very carefully to what the participant does own and know and then draw it out for exploration and learning.

This technique has to be used cautiously, especially with adult groups. The intention is not to "trick" the participant, but to bypass the internal critic preventing him/her from "knowing." You could end up having the following exchange:

Facilitator: Why do you think most people sit in the same place every day at lunch?

Participant: I don't know.

Facilitator: What if you did know?

Participant: I just told you, I don't know!

When this happens, we have learned to smile and respond, "Great ... take a guess." It is amazing what good guessers most people are.

* The bottom line for this kind of inquiry is to stay committed. "What if you did know?" and "Guess" are really just code language for, "I really care about you and am honestly interested

in what you have to say." By not allowing a participant to get away with, "I don't know" when they truly do have some ability to answer, the facilitator moves conversation forward and builds trust in the group.

Gate-Keep

Gate-keeping is noticing the people who are quiet or shy and have not participated in the conversation. The facilitator can open the gate for a person to speak. At the right moment, you might direct a question to the quiet one. "Monica, what do you think about people supporting each other in the work place?" Don't get hung up on whether the person chooses to answer the question. What's important is making sure everyone has the opportunity to share.

You can even lead into this gently by saying, "I haven't heard much from some of you, would someone who hasn't spoken yet tell us what you are thinking or feeling?" This kind of gentle invitation is all that is necessary sometimes.

Boomerang

Often in the early stages of a group's processing time, participants ask questions of and make comments to the facilitator rather than directly address one another. It is the facilitator's job to help the group communicate with each other as directly as possible.

Boomeranging is the art of giving a question or statement back to the group for consideration and comments, rather than commenting on and answering them yourself. The more challenging the question, observation, or statement, the more likely it will be directed toward the facilitator. This is because it can be easier to

give away authority and knowledge than to risk owning it. The
challenge of the facilitator is to send the question, observation,
or statement back to the group for pondering and exploration.

> Facilitator: Did you notice that, as a group, you all
> looked to Pete for leadership? (Question 1)
> Group: Yeah.
> Facilitator: Why did that happen? (Question 2)
> Participant: I'm not sure ... uh, is that common for
> groups to do?
> Facilitator: That's a good question; what do you all
> think about that?

Another scenario for boomeranging in the context of
The 5 Questions could also look like this:

> Facilitator: Did you notice, as a group, you all looked
> to Simon for leadership? (Question 1)
> Group: Yeah.
> Facilitator: Why did that happen? (Question 2)
> Participant 1: I think it's because we are not that good
> at working together, and so Simon just took over.
> Facilitator: Is that true at work? (Question 3)
> Group: Yeah.
> Facilitator: Why does this happen?
> Participant 2: Because when a group can't figure out
> what to do to be a better team, I think it starts looking
> for help or someone to be in charge so, at least, the
> work can get done.
> Facilitator: What do you all think about that? Is it true
> we naturally want someone else to be in charge when
> we can't figure it out on our own?

Instead of going straight to Question 5, the facilitator put Participant 2's comment out to the group and asked for input on the observation without asserting her own opinion. It is important for you as the facilitator to pay attention. Are you answering/responding to more questions than the group? If so, use the boomerang technique, and send those questions back to the group.

Reframing

When a group gets particularly stuck or conflict feels too hard, use your perspective as an outsider to reframe the issue. For example, imagine a group stuck on whether cooperation or competition will achieve the best result. As you listen to the exchange of ideas, you may see a middle way that enables the group to get unstuck—reframing the issue away from either/or to both/and. For example, "Instead of competing or cooperating, could aspects of both have relevance?"

When participants get fixated on small issues, the facilitator can help by zooming out on the issue and reframing the problem in the context of what is best for the big picture. We have seen groups get hung up on a single rule they felt was unfair. "It wasn't fair that we couldn't see the game board and they could! That was why they were so much faster." In this context, we can reframe the issue in a bigger way to help the group move forward. "Why do you think the rules were set up that way? Does it highlight a particular aspect of working together?"

Alternatively, you can reframe by zooming in. For example, a group is going in circles about what effective leadership should look like. The facilitator can reframe by asking the group to think about a particular work context. Framing the conversation through the viewpoint of a project manager, verses the viewpoint of the division president, can have a dramatic impact on the way the group understands the situation. As a facilitator, your task is to frame the issues in a way that works for the group and promotes understanding on all sides.

What If

Another favorite techniques is to ask, "What if ...?" It has so many varied and interesting applications; we challenge you to look for appropriate places to insert it.

"What if ...?" is just a plain, powerful question. It helps participants explore different angles of the topic at hand. "What if ..." questions invite the group to notice what didn't happen in a particular scenario and, as a result, ponder alternative possibilities.

- What if you all cooperated?
- What if you had asked for outside support?
- What if you attempted this entirely by yourself?

Dichotomies

Is that good or bad? Did that help or hurt? Are you moving forward or backward? Contrasts force people to choose and then explore why they chose what they did. Differing opinions open the opportunity for participants to take a stand on an issue and then explore their rationale.

We like introducing an either/or choice in the generalization aspect (Question 3 or 4). This is when participants are grappling with the significance of the learning in which they are engaged. Notice the following exchange:

> Facilitator: Did you notice I never assigned teams? (Question 1)
> Participant: That's right, you never did; we just formed teams on our own!
> Facilitator: Why did that happen? (Question 2)
> Participant: Well, it seemed like there were limited resources, so we just organized ourselves in a way that would allow us to win the simulation.
> Facilitator: Does that happen in life? (Question 3)
> Participant: Absolutely. We often align ourselves to compete when we perceive resources are limited.
> Facilitator: Is that good or bad? (Dichotomy)

Having generalized the experience, we can ask participants to delve into the notion of whether they are engaging in behaviors they want to continue. This can lead to fascinating and powerful conversations. At the same time, we realize this kind of forced dichotomy is not always appropriate. Few choices are truly either/or, and the world is full of shades of gray.

Accept/Legitimize/Deal With/Defer

Negative comments and distractions are the most difficult things to handle as a facilitator. In approaching these potential roadblocks, we recognize four available responses. First, you can **accept** it. Sometimes by accepting the world as it presents itself, warts and all, you can move past it. Accepting a negative comment is essentially to do nothing. You give minimal response, simply accept the comment was made, and move on.

To **legitimize** is to give a positive response to a negative situation. Call it out and acknowledge the reality of the situation. For example, a student says, "This is stupid." You agree wholeheartedly with, "Yes, this is really stupid." This counter-intuitive response can often take a negative person by surprise. By legitimizing the complaint, you may be able to open the person to seeing that although s/he is right, s/he may not be paying attention to the whole picture.

To **deal with** a negative comment requires additional tools and time. The decision to take on a negative comment or situation, sets you up for a battle, and in some cases, there can only be one winner. Proceed with extreme caution when directly confronting a negative person.

To **defer** negativity can often be the most effective strategy, especially when pressed for time. Our advice is to trust the process. Often participants who start out negative or resistant eventually come to see enormous value in the conversation. Some even become active participants. When you defer, you need to trust the negativity will not infect the rest of the group and the process will work to shift the negative participants.

Humor

Laughter is a powerful, unifying force in any group. Humor can cut through tension and shift the energy dramatically. We encourage you to use it! If humor doesn't come naturally to you, then become adept at noticing the inborn humor and fabulous absurdity of life found in almost any group or situation at some point.

It is important to avoid humor that is sarcastic or at someone's expense, especially as a facilitator. Damage to group trust happens quickly, and, once done, it is difficult to repair.

Get Up and Move

There are times when the conversation has gone on so long and been so intense that participants just need to get up and move around in order to refocus and reenergize. Give them permission to get up and stretch.

Play a quick game, do crazy kinetics—such as jumping jacks or a hand jive, switching chairs or places in the circle, or just running around the room. Get the blood flowing and the ideas will again flow freely.

Take a Break

Sometimes just moving around isn't enough to get the group refocused. Take a break and come back to the topic after people have a chance to get some food, go to the bathroom, walk around a bit, etc. It's important to pay attention and take care of the group in this way. On the other hand, use breaks judiciously. Once the group breaks, it can be difficult to pull them back. Before letting them go, give a restart time and be prepared to walk around and pull them back to the circle when it's time to start again.

Dialogue

One last thing we want to mention before ending this chapter is dialogue. Dialogue is a process for conversation aptly described by physicist David Bohm (1996), among others. Bohm defines dialogue as a process to use with groups to help people understand others' and their own thoughts.

The process often leads to uncovering deeply held assumptions about culture, meaning, and identity.

It is our hope that after reading this book and using The 5 Questions, you will be curious to learn more about facilitation and deeply transformative conversation. The process of good dialogue can teach us much about how to listen to and engage in powerful conversation with one another. A few of the key concepts used in dialogue are listed here to provoke interest.

Suspend Your Own Beliefs and Assumptions

Invite participants to really explore how the person speaking arrived at his/her belief. Encourage them to more deeply hear and potentially understand one another. This is a challenging objective, and when you are successful, the level of discovery and exploration that results is awesome.

Balance Inquiry With Advocacy

Advocacy is when you put energy toward explaining your own point of view or experience. Inquiry is when you suspend your own views and actively seek to understand someone else's point of view. In dialogue, participants should be aware of the roles of advocacy and inquiry, the intention being to balance between the two and learn what each mode feels and looks like. In this way, we can actually have dialogue, instead of two monologues taking place back and forth.

Welcome and Explore Different Points of View

By discovering/discerning our differences, we learn more about one another. This is still an uncommon approach to divergent thinking, and it is exciting when groups learn to welcome thinking that is not similar. Amazing new pathways to creativity and learning open.

Enjoy the Process—Dialogue Can Be Playful and Fun!

This is part of our attraction to dialogue as a process. It's deep and transformational, and it's fun! There are dialogue groups all over the country, and many books about the process are available. We hope you are curious to discover more about dialogue. Please refer to the bibliography for more information.

Chapter Five

We Need an Outcome!

The important thing is not to stop questioning.
Curiosity has its own reason for existing.
—Albert Einstein

The premise that learning is best, most fun, and lasts longest when facilitators and educators are truly open to outcome is foundational to this book and this method. When learners are able to arrive at the meaning and lessons that are right for them at that time, then those lessons are the strongest.

Sometimes, however, we do not have that luxury. Most educators have content that students need to learn, and many facilitators are charged with achieving certain objectives with clients. Can The 5 Questions model still work when you have a specific agenda in mind? Yes, absolutely.

As with all methods, there are pros and cons to using The 5 Questions to achieve specific outcomes. First, it is worth thinking about other available methods. Does this content require a lecture? Lectures are a time-efficient means to deliver a lot of information. Lectures can be especially appropriate when combined with experience and practice. It's even possible to reflect on a lecture experience by having students think about what they heard and how the lecture applies to what they are meant to be learning.

That said, our collective experience continues to validate that lecturing remains one of the least effective means of getting students to retain information. Think about the many lectures you have sat through in your life. How many of them do you remember? Of the ones you do remember, how much of the lecture do you actually remember? The more immersive the experience, that is to say the more senses we engage, the more likely the information is to be retained.

This brings us back to various kinds of experiences. When it is important that students retain the information, we want to engage them in some way beyond a lecture. Just engaging students will increase the amount of information retained, but to really have content become cemented in long term memory, it must go through those 5 stages of learning we talked about in chapter one: Experience, Describe, Interpret, Generalize, and Apply.

The 5 Questions therefore becomes a particularly useful way to direct learning when students need to learn particular content. To get the most effective and time-efficient conversation going, there are several steps that can be particularly helpful.

Be Clear About the Objectives

So often we begin a lesson with some vague idea about what we want students to learn. This is a perfect mind-set when you are open to outcome. If you have a vague sense of direction, but are still open to where your group takes the conversation, then you are ready for anything. If, however, you have a specific objective in mind, you had better be clear and exact in your understanding of the objective. Are you building on past lessons or attempting to redirect or expand upon past group behavior?

Micah was hired to do a workshop on presentation skills with a group of non-profit executives. The person hosting the training specifically let him know the group had expressed confidence in the material they were to present, but felt uncomfortable speaking in front of their peer group. With this knowledge in mind, Micah was able to focus the experiences he designed and the processing of each experience with the single objective of increasing confidence and security when working with and presenting to a group of peers. Had he generically focused on the whole range of "presentation skills," the training would have had much less efficacy.

What are you trying to achieve? How specific does your objective need to be? Is this a content training or lesson? Do students need to master the quadratic equation or is this just a session to increase their sense of trust and camaraderie? Knowing specifically what you are trying to achieve is the best way to deliver your message in a timely and effective manner, so that no time is wasted.

Front-Load the Challenge

Front-loading is a technique of focusing attention. Our attention has several predictable cues. We automatically notice movement, sharp loud sounds, and bright colors. For our particular purpose, we have an amazing capacity to observe what we consciously direct our attention toward. For instance, if I simply ask you to think about breakfast this morning, it is almost impossible for your brain not to flicker backward in time to breakfast. Just mentioning the word "breakfast" sends our synapses back in time to reflect that event, even if it was not in our consciousness at all a moment ago.

This works the same with our students. If we ask them to focus their attention somewhere before they even engage in the experience, it is next to impossible for them not to notice what we asked of them. For example, focus your students' attention in a generic way by saying, "In this next activity, please pay careful attention to ...

- teamwork
- leadership
- conflict
- communication
- winners and losers
- decision-making
- feelings
- participation"

← What are we going to learn

In this way, before the experience even begins, you have directed the focus of their attention. Then you can simply start the reflection process with the "Did you notice ...?" that corresponds to that topic. "Okay, so did you notice the level of teamwork you exhibited?"

This kind of generic-directed attention works really well for groups working on what are sometimes referred to as "soft skills." Could you use this same technique for teaching "hard skills" within a particular academic area?

Absolutely. Just front-load the observation that will lead toward the lesson you need students to learn.

- "In this next exercise/practice/worksheet/film, I want you to pay particular attention to...
  - The angles within each of the triangles
  - The way the denominator works
  - The particular issues that drove the factions to war
  - The way the character is set up for a tragic fall
  - How the chemical reaction differs from what we saw last week
  - Which verbs are irregular."

Front-loading an experience with directed attention focuses participants on particular observations, which will often lead them into the lesson we need them to retain.

Design the Experience

How can you maximize the learning in a tight time frame with specific objectives? Design the experience to direct attention and learning in a singular direction. This is easy to say; however, it might be the most difficult thing in this book to do—far, far more difficult than processing an experience or setting up casual fun. Designing compact, engaging, and directed learning can be a challenge for even the most experienced leaders.

Think about some of the most incredible experiences of your life for a moment. How many of them were directed lessons? For most people there aren't very many experiences like that. Think now about favorite teachers. Do any particular lessons stand out as unforgettable?

For Micah, it was his second-grade teacher, Mr. Bell, who created the first "forever" learning experience. Mr. Bell began with an incredible front-load. He said, "Class, tomorrow it is important that every single one of you bring an umbrella." There was almost no chance it was going to rain (Micah grew up in the high desert), so the students were confused. Mr. Bell followed up by saying he was going to make it rain indoors, and if they wanted to make sure they didn't get wet, they should bring an umbrella.

Talk about excitement and directed attention. For some of the kids, it was all they could think about that night. Many of the kids brought umbrellas the next day, and Mr. Bell let them know this was a one-time exception to the "never open an umbrella indoors" rule. So up went the umbrellas.

Mr. Bell then began heating a pot of water on a Bunsen burner. Next, he took a cold frying pan out of the cooler he had brought that day and placed it directly above the boiling water. He narrated to the class each step of the way, and when the steam from the boiling water condensed on the cold pan above it, and a single drip of water fell back into the pot, Mr. Bell proudly announced that we had just seen it rain indoors.

Mr. Bell quickly moved forward with his own intuitive set of questions (that very much mirrored The 5 Questions), leading the students to reflect on what they had seen. Micah still thinks of that cold frying pan whenever he sees condensation! The lesson was incredibly focused, very direct, and led perfectly into the learning.

How do we do that when it's not quite so obvious? How do you design experiences for abstract learnings like "thinking ahead" or "being nice to everyone"? Even more difficult, how do we design experiences to teach state mandated standards in subject areas like math, social studies, and language arts? Can you design experiences for any kind of learning?

Ultimately, yes. An experience or demonstration can be created for just about any learning objective. The challenge is that designing experiences is MUCH more involved than simply giving a lecture or assigning reading. Not only is it more work, it also takes more time. There is that constant trade-off between efficiency and effectiveness again. How much time in your program should participants or students spend sitting and listening? How much time should they be involved in an active experience? How much time do you need to process the experience? There is no easy answer to this set of questions.

Some have suggested simple models like 20-60-20 to make programming easier, breaking up the time available into 20% lecture, 60% experience, and 20% debrief/reflection. While handy for some environments, this kind of easy solution can be sadly inadequate in the face of real world constraints on time, varying degrees of importance in the material, and interest/capability of the participants.

The bottom line is, if you know what you want your group to learn, it is always possible to design an experience to highlight that learning, make it easier to understand, and ensure it is retained by your students longer.

Know Where to Focus

So, how do you actually design experiences that will translate into learning? Alternatively, when using experiences designed by others (there are hundreds of resources to help with this, see Additional Resources for a good starter list), how do you make sure your participants get the right kind of learning out of that experience?

Clearly, this begins with an exact understanding of your objectives. Because we are attempting to speak to a wide variety of practitioners through this book, it is difficult to speak too specifically about objectives without quickly going down content areas. So, we will speak generally about a couple of ideas, then give two examples to help make it clear how to hone in on your learning objectives.

When thinking through your learning objectives, it is best to begin with broad concepts and then try to isolate the specific components of that concept. Start with the main theme or standard you are aiming to teach (e.g., teamwork, communication skills, ratios, plot development, causes for civil wars). Then try to separate the pieces/steps that make up the whole. As you start to figure out exactly what you want participants to learn, it will be easier to design a focused experience to grab their attention.

So, for instance, if you are working with a group on teamwork, isolate the specific learning you want to target as you design the experience and prepare for reflection. On what aspect of teamwork do you want to focus? Teamwork has dozens of component skills or ideas:

- cooperating versus competing
- awareness of others contributions
- speaking your mind/sharing your ideas
- listening to others
- following the rules
- knowing when to break the rules

- compromise
- patience and follow through

So, let's imagine you are working with a group that needs to focus more on listening to each other. Rather than setting up a generic exercise for teamwork like Team Juggling and hoping they notice something about listening in the course of it, design an experience that requires participants to focus on listening, like Coaching Walk.

Team Juggling

A variation of a classic experiential education game (Rohnke, 1984)

SAY THIS

"Okay group, let's get in a circle. I'm going to hand one of you a bean bag. Once you have the bean bag, toss it to someone else in the circle and say his/her name. Make sure you have their attention first, and try to include everyone in the circle."

DO THIS

Hand the bean bag to a participant and let the group play round one. After 1 minute, collect the bean bag.

SAY THIS

"Now that you have that pretty well figured out, let's see what happens when I increase the challenge. I am going to introduce 2 more bean bags. The rules are the same, except now 3 bean bags will be tossed around the circle at the same time."

Do This

Watch—with most groups, the increase in bean bags quickly creates chaos. Add more or take away bean bags, help them strategize, or do whatever you think will help the experience to be enlightening. Close with The 5 Questions.

Coaching Walk

Do This

Have everyone partner up in whatever way you like.

Say This

"With your partner, quickly decide who will be the coach and who will be the walker first. Walkers, when we start, you will close your eyes completely. You won't open them until you reach your destination. Where you decide to go will be up to you. In a moment, I will have you tell your coach specifically where in the room you want to go.

"Coaches, you will be able to see and talk to your walkers, but you may not touch them or move anything out of their way. You may only use your voice to communicate.

"Okay, Walkers, tell your partner where you would like to go in the room and then close your eyes. Coaches, get your walker there safely!"

Do This

Watch everyone for safety. When walkers reach their destinations, have the partners switch roles. Process the experience using The 5 Questions.

With the Coaching Walk activity, we have taken lots of stimulation away so participants can think exclusively about listening. However, there are still a lot of other experiences that might catch their attention. With their eyes closed, they might get hung up on safety issues or the mechanics of walking blind.

The more clearly you can design an experience to isolate just the lesson you are trying to highlight, the more likely participants and students will notice it and learn from it. Keep in mind, however, that no matter how perfectly you set it up, they will notice the things most relevant to them.

Maybe designing the experience seems straightforward for concepts like teamwork and leadership, but becomes more difficult when dealing with academic subjects. Truly, it is the same process but with the focus on highlighting the components within the heart of every academic subject. Ultimately, all academics are an attempt to understand the world and our place in it. To that end, everything we formally teach in school has been built upon the observations and experiences of generations before us. When we can bring students into that same moment of discovery, we can make even the driest of subjects more interesting and relevant.

So let's imagine you are attempting to teach something like fiction as a source of information about the real world. The assigned text is *The Great Gatsby*. As a standard, you need your students to discover their own real life connections to the plot and characters present in the novel. Of course, you could use The 5 Questions to simply get students to pay attention to certain aspects of the book (i.e., "Do you notice that Nick Carraway is a silent narrator throughout *The Great Gatsby* even though he witnesses crime, betrayal, and backstabbing? ... Why do you think he stays silent?")

Even more powerful than simply calling attention to specific aspects of the book, however, would be designing an experience to immerse students in their own exploration of the novel. For instance, to highlight that Nick Carraway is a silent narrator and that people in real life often stay silent in the face of challenging situations, you might design an experience that highlights that behavior using Lived Monopoly.

Lived Monopoly

Do This

Make a simulated Monopoly board. Maybe change the space names to streets or places from The Great Gatsby. Divide students into teams. Play accelerated rounds to speed up the game. Have the banker (which could be you or a student team) arbitrarily award two or three teams extra money in each round. When students complain that this is unfair, do nothing and instruct the game to continue.

Close with The 5 Questions, calling attention to silent observation, disparity, and criminal behavior.

What about math? Can you help students experience mathematics? Again, without question, the answer is yes. There are many modern math educators advocating immersive problem-solving within mathematics. We are starting to understand that mathematical thinking has less to do with getting the right answers and more to do with thinking about and developing good strategies for solving problems. Let's say you wanted to teach this very important concept/standard to students of almost any grade level. By immersing students in an activity like Fast Fingers (see page 127) you can direct their attention specifically to the issue of multiple strategies.

The conversation might start like this:

Teacher: Did you notice that some of you created strategies to be more successful? (Question 1)
Students: Yes!
Teacher: Will someone volunteer what strategy they used?
Student 1: I just put out no fingers each time so that I only had to count their fingers.
Teacher: Why was that successful? (Question 2)
Student 1: It made the problem a lot simpler for me!
Teacher: Did someone else use a different strategy? (Question 1)
Student 2: Yeah! I put my fingers into weird combinations not normally used to display the number 4. It totally worked because they had a hard time counting my fingers, while I could easily count theirs!
Teacher: Do you notice that different strategies could be equally successful here? (Question 1)
Students: Yes, of course!
Teacher: Do you think the same thing is true in solving math problems? (Question 3)

Important in all three of these examples (teamwork, *The Great Gatsby*, and multiple strategies in math) is the implicit understanding that you can generate a higher level of engagement and more lasting learning by 1) knowing what you are trying to get students to learn, 2) focusing on the sub-skills or concepts within that general concept, and 3) then designing an experience to highlight those sub-skills or concepts.

Key Concepts in Designing Experience

1. **Patterns of Behavior:** How will students likely behave in this experience? If possible, run a demo of the experience with a group to get a sense of the behaviors it creates.

2. **Attention Demanders:** Think about where the students' attention is most likely to fall. Remember that we are tuned to notice specific sensations: movement, bright colors, loud sounds. We are also highly tuned to notice certain emotions: anger, frustration, surprise, fear. Does the experience generate any of those things in a predictable way that can be used to focus students' attention?

3. **Work Backwards:** Imagine the end of The 5 Questions (What will you do now?) How do you hope students will respond? "I will listen more carefully in team conversations and learn to trust that generally we all want to keep each other safe." "I will research inequity in our society and compare it to the society portrayed in Gatsby." "I will try more than one strategy when I get stuck on a problem and remember the answer is less important than learning effective processes." Once you have determined what the end could sound like, work backwards step-by-step to see how you might

generate a conversation leading to that conclusion. What observations need to be present for that kind of discussion? Based on those observations, what kind of experience do you need to design?

Your First "Did You Notice ...?"

Have you noticed the importance of that first "Did you notice ...?" question? It is critical. It has the impact of taking the forest of sensations that participants have just experienced and honing in like a laser on just a single tree. We cannot overstate the power and importance of this question.

Of course, "Did you notice ...?" is important when trying to stay open to outcome, but it is absolutely critical when you are trying to deliver a predetermined lesson. Where you direct participants' attention determines how interesting, relevant, and ultimately, how smoothly your reflection process will go.

The difficulty in writing about developing excellent "Did you notice ...?" questions is that there is no guide. We can't give you a formula for crafting perfect questions because the best questions are anchored in the actual experience of the participants and drive smoothly toward a waiting lesson. We can say that all the tips mentioned in chapter three are still relevant for crafting good questions, even when you are attempting to deliver a specific lesson. To generate an engaged conversation anchor your "Did you notice ...?" question in behavior and emotion.

Notice the Trends

In addition, take advantage of observable trends in your groups. When developing an experience that can be used with multiple groups, you begin to notice the behavior trends. For instance, Micah runs the activity Fast Fingers (see page 127) frequently with many different groups. Because he has led it and played it many times, he knows that as he sets up the activity, many people immediately say to themselves, "This is math so I am going to be terrible at it." What a self-defeating thought—however, he has seen that behavior show up time after time. So if Micah wants to teach a lesson on changing self-talk to be more positive, he can simply ask, "Did you notice that you said to yourself, 'This is math, I'll probably be terrible at it and lose'?"

With that simple first question, he has taken all the different thoughts, feelings, and observations—"My partner is really fast," "They keep putting out no fingers!" "The clock on the wall has the wrong time," "I keep looking at the instructor to tell me if I'm right"—and focused them down to one simple observation: Be aware of your internal self-talk.

By taking advantage of observable and experienced trends in activities and simulations, you can eventually start to predict exactly what kind of question will lead most efficiently to the lesson you are trying to teach.

New Experiences

What if you have never done this lesson before? Then take your best guess. Just by asking questions rather than simply lecturing you have already increased the likelihood your participants will have a more meaningful experience. Trust yourself and stay aware of your group.

If your first question doesn't generate the response you are searching for, listen carefully to how the group and individual participants do respond. Maybe your observation of their experience was off. Alternatively, maybe they didn't really listen to your question. Allow yourself the curiosity and humility to start over again and again if necessary. Continue to refocus the group down the line of questioning that is most likely to lead to the lesson you need to teach.

Connect the Dots

One of the most challenging things about not being open to outcome in a conversation is recognizing when you have made connections your participants have not yet made. The path toward learning seems so obvious to you. It's right there in front of them!

As a facilitator or teacher, we often see concepts so frequently, or engage in experiences so easily, it is difficult to remember how we first encountered the material that is now second-nature. Even if we remember our first discoveries, they are just that, OUR discoveries. We all discover things at our own pace and in our own way. The path that brought us to the things we believe to be true may not be the same path anyone else would take.

When you are facilitating with an end in mind, stay really focused on listening carefully to what participants are saying. What connections are they making? When you ask for examples in question 4, "Where do you see this happening," what kinds of connections to their lives are they making?

When a group or participant makes connection that are off-track from the lesson you are trying to teach, see if you can backtrack to their line of thinking. What observation did they make that led them to this connection? What interpretation have they made around that observation?

If needed, you can connect the dots more directly. Let's imagine you are trying to use the Fast Fingers activity to teach about positive and negative self-talk. You start in the way we discussed earlier:

> Facilitator: "Did you notice you said to yourself in the beginning, "This is math, so I probably won't be very good at it?" (Question 1)
> Group: (Many, but not all, nod their heads.)
> Facilitator: Why do you think you did that? (Question 2)
> Participant: I am always bad at math. No surprise there! (laughs)

This participant wants to make a connection to his skill level rather than the internal dialogue in his head. At this point, the facilitator can redirect the group to focus on the internal dialogue.

> Facilitator: Okay, I hear what you are saying about being bad at math but I'm really interested in what you said to yourself before we played Fast Fingers. Raise your hand if you remember saying to yourself "I'm going to be bad at this …" for whatever reason?
> Group: (Many raise their hand.)
> Facilitator: Okay, interesting. Many of you are acknowledging that thought. Now I wonder, do you think that thought helped make you better at the

activity or somehow made you worse? (Question 1—dichotomy)

Group: It probably made us worse.

Facilitator: Okay, great. I thought you might say that, which raises a really good question. Whether or not you are bad at math, you thought something in your head that made you actually perform worse. Why would you allow yourself to do that? (Refocused Question 2)

In this way, the facilitator helps the group to hone in and focus on just the observation and ultimately the learning toward which s/he is driving. This is certainly a skill that facilitators need to develop. The more you practice refocusing a group and driving in on certain points, the more seamless it will become.

Stay Open

Of course we can't leave this topic without one last appeal to STAY OPEN! The high stakes environment where most of us work means we all have objectives we have to reach. Students have to take tests. Groups need measurable objectives for team-building sessions. Even campers need to return home with certain objectives achieved to ensure parents see the value of their investment. In so much of our work, we have to be focused. We get it.

However ... maybe, just maybe, in our quest to reach continuous objectives, we miss a certain wandering. Maybe we close off the learning when we are just on the brink of crashing through the walls of resistance. Maybe by forcing students to march down our path, we rob them of the joy inherent in exploring their own path.

Whenever you can, stay open. Watch the actual experience of your students, participants, and groups. Really watch. As you observe, stay curious and interested along with them. And, if that golden moment should occur where you see a student on the brink of a new discovery, see if you can patiently allow that relevant learning to come forward. Those will be, without a doubt, the most powerful moments for your participants. They will also be the most powerful for you.

Chapter Six | **Make It Experiential!**

"It's not the same to talk of bulls, as to be in the bullring."
—Spanish Proverb

How many times have we watched an earnest presenter stand and lecture about how important it is for participants to **experience** their learning? We believe it is imperative to teach reflection and closure through experience. Better to memorize and practice The 5 Questions in the safe confines of a workshop than during a live reflection discussion.

We have taught The 5 Questions to thousands of new facilitators—young and old, experienced and inexperienced. In fact, every fall, over 500,000 high school and middle school facilitators use The 5 Questions method to help create meaning around activities for freshmen and 6th graders during their transitions into a new school. The activities and workshop presented in this chapter were developed in support of the Link Crew and WEB programs. We are deeply indebted to these programs for giving us a reason to create The 5 Questions and allowing us the space and time to develop and refine them over the last 20 years.

i swear i lived

I swear I lived

The 5 Questions workshop was designed for beginning facilitators, although we have used it with more advanced facilitators as well. Camp counselors, outdoor experience facilitators, teachers, counselors, and staff-development professionals will all find this workshop beneficial. When a group already has a functional understanding of the learning cycle and/or other questioning methodologies like Bloom's Taxonomy or Socratic Dialog, then the conversation about how The 5 Questions might be useful can be extremely rich.

This workshop is designed to be conducted in a 60- to 90-minute block. Like you, we are often time-constrained in our work and always seek to make the most impact in the least amount of time possible. A certain degree of pacing and timing is required to combine engaged fun in the moment with long-lasting impact. We have borrowed the activities we use in these workshops from a wide variety of sources. This book is not intended to be an experiential activities and games book.

Building in some level of assessment is helpful when working with new facilitators who will shortly be responsible for using this material. **Assessing a facilitator's skill** is one of the most challenging aspects of teaching this methodology. Many people tend to overestimate their skill in facilitation. As we have few models of how it ought to look, and each experience is distinct from the previous one, determining mastery can be difficult. Finding a way to observe and provide immediate feedback to new facilitators is critical. We highly encourage a program of observation to ensure your teaching is actually being learned and applied. Brain research reveals the old adage is true: *Practice does not make perfect; perfect practice makes perfect* (Vince Lombardi).

* The longer a new facilitator goes without feedback to improve,
* the more likely s/he will get stuck in non-productive patterns.

The 5 Questions Workshop Outline

Introduction

Activity: Hand Slap (classic folk game)
* Setup
* Play
* Guided reflection

Lecture: The Power of Setting Up Learning

Lecture: The 5 Questions
* First step – memorize

Activity: Orchestra
* Memorizing activity

Activity: Quiz
* Memorizing activity

Activity: Fast Fingers (Rohnke, 1984)
* Choose teams of 3, designate A, B, & C
* A guides reflection, B & C play

Lecture: Noticing

Activity: Push Pull (classic folk game)
* B guides reflection, A & C play

Lecture: Genuine Curiosity

Activity: Gotcha (Rohnke, 1984)
* C guides reflection, A & B play

Activity: Count Off (Rohnke, 1984)
* Groups of 8 practice, designate 1 to guide reflection

The 5 Questions Workshop

PURPOSE: Teach The 5 Questions methodology and allow participants an opportunity to practice

TIME REQUIRED: 60-90 minutes (depending on the size and experience of the group)

MATERIALS REQUIRED: None

Introduction •

MAIN POINTS
- Introduce the workshop.
- Prepare for experiences.

SAY THIS

"Welcome to the fun of processing experiential activities. Our objective in the next hour is to provide you with the basic framework for asking great questions as well as the opportunity to practice your skill. We cannot do a workshop about experience without having a few experiences, so with that brief introduction, let's get started."

Activity: Hand Slap • • • • • • • • • • • • • • • •

PROCEDURE

"Please stand up and choose a partner." (Use any method of pairing people that you wish—keep time constraints in mind.) "Once you have a partner, please stand facing each other. One partner place both hands palms up about waist high. The other person now place your hands, palms down, over your partner's. You should now be palm to palm.

"Ready. Go." (Carefully observe the reaction of the group when you say "go." Do not give further instructions. After a few minutes, get the group's attention again.)

"Go ahead and sit down. Please turn to your partner and talk about that experience for a moment. What did you notice as you were playing?" (Let the pairs discuss for a few minutes.)

QUESTIONS

- Did you notice I did not actually tell you which game to play? (Question 1)
- Why did most of you play the same game? (Question 2)
- Does that happen in life? (Question 3)
- Where does that happen? (Question 4)
- What will you do now you are aware of that? (Question 5)

Note: This is a guided reflection much as we discuss in chapter five. As we are in more of a training mentality, we are not as open to outcome as we might be during a more open experience. Here it is helpful for participants to notice that experience guides action, and by setting the group up in a particular way, you get a more predictable response.

After the group responds to The 5 Questions, ask the following series of questions:

QUESTIONS

- Did you notice we are no longer talking about the game Hand Slap? (Question 1)

- What are we talking about? (Question 1 - variation)
- Why are we talking about that, and not the game Hand Slap? (Question 2)
- Do you think guided questions can lead other groups to interesting insights and learning for other experiences? (Question 3)
- I hoped you might see that as well. Let's take a moment to look specifically at the questions I asked and how they work.

Lecture: The Power of Setting Up Learning • • •

MAIN POINTS

- Setup can predict outcome.
- Use setup to ask the right questions at the right times.

SAY THIS

"The setup was critical for this activity, right? Part of our success as facilitators is our ability to set up experiences that will enable people to reflect on their actions and feelings. Notice that how you set up learning can often predict the kind of learning experience you will have. The setup is critical.

"As facilitators, our job is to set up our groups to be reflective and engaged about their own learning. We are not necessarily going to tell them what to learn, just as in this last activity, I didn't tell you what to play. Rather, we are going to create an environment for learning, ask questions that make it possible, and then guide our groups toward powerful connections."

Lecture: The 5 Questions • • • • • • • • • • • •

MAIN POINTS

- You must first memorize these questions in order to be able to use them effectively later.

    1)   Did you notice ... ?
    2)   Why did that happen?
    3)   Does that happen in life?
    4)   Who? What? Where? When? Why?
    5)   What will you do now?

SAY THIS

"To help set up learning, we need to learn five critical questions. These questions are mapped against how the brain processes and learns from experience. When asked with the right degree of skill, they unlock the learning potential in each of the experiences we will do with our groups.

The 5 Questions are:
1)   Did you notice ... ?
2)   Why did that happen?
3)   Does that happen in life?
4)   Who? What? Where? When? Why?
5)   What will you do now?

"Each of these questions works together to help groups connect their experiences with each other to the experience of their lives. These connections create the environment for learning.

"Consider a little boy who burns his hand by touching a hot pot on a stove. He first notices the pain in his hand. He immediately starts to wonder why and thinks about the pot. Correctly making the connection between the hot pot and the pain in his hand allows him to consider that all hot things, especially when they are on a stove, might cause pain. This generalization will now guide his future experience with hot things. Hopefully he will no longer touch them. By consciously visiting each of these points on the 'learning cycle,' we help our groups create their own meaning from experience.

"Now let's turn our attention to actually memorizing these questions."

Activity: Orchestra • • • • • • • • • • • • • • • •

PROCEDURE

"Music is a powerful tool for memorizing. Notice how you can hear a song on the radio and have it stuck in your head for hours afterward? We are going to use the power of song to help us remember The 5 Questions. Each question will have its own tune."

"First up is, 'Did you notice ... ?'" (Use an operatic style, or make up a tune that works for you.)

"Let's practice. When I point to you, sing out loud!" (They sing.) "Great first attempt; now let's do it with real gusto! Again!" (They sing louder.)

"Okay great, now the second question, 'Why did that happen?'" (Use a jazzy, low key, finger-snapping style.)

"Now the third question, 'Does it happen in life?'" (Use a rap/hip hop motif.)

"Now the fourth question, 'Who? What? Where? When? Why?'" (Make this a repetitive deep, booming chant.)

"Finally, the fifth question, our capstone, 'What will you do now?'" (Use a pounding rocker melody complete with air guitar. [We are indebted to our colleague Mary Beth Campbell for enlightening us to the simplicity and utter ferocity of the rocker/air guitar riff. You may encourage your group to hit the whammy bar on their guitar and scream the last word.])

"Now that everyone knows the tunes, I am going to divide the group into five sections. Each section will take a different question, and I will conduct our 5 Questions masterpiece!" (Give all five groups a chance to practice their piece, then you conduct the orchestra. Have the groups go one at a time so everyone gets to hear and appreciate each question.)

"Give yourselves a round of applause. Phenomenal music was just made! Mentally review each of The 5 Questions to see if they have begun to sink in."

Activity: Quiz

PROCEDURE

"The real test as to whether you have learned The 5 Questions will be if you can accurately remember them tomorrow. However, just to see if you are on the way, here comes a pop quiz!

"Please stand and give us question #1." (Point to one participant at random.)

"Group, let's give them a thunderous applause!! I mean really ridiculously over-the-top applause!!"

Ask people at random to stand and recite one of the questions. Gently correct them if they are wrong—in our experience they are rarely incorrect at this point, especially with other group members whispering the answer if they seem to be struggling. Continue to provide overwhelming applause to reinforce the fun and safety of this impromptu quiz.

Finally, ask one or two people to recite the entire 5 Questions in order. Give these people a standing ovation.

Activity: Fast Fingers • • • • • • • • • • • • • • •

PROCEDURE

"Now that you know The 5 Questions in order, we need to give you an opportunity to practice with them. Please get into groups of three, and designate a person 'A,' a person 'B,' and a person 'C.'

"Person A, for this first activity you will be the observer and then you will simply ask as many "Did you notice ...?" questions as possible. That means you need to pay attention to the activity as your partners are playing. Notice their interaction, their feelings, and their behaviors. Any one of these things might be a good source for you to use with 'Did you notice ...?'

"B and C, you will play Fast Fingers. First, put both hands behind your back. On the count of three, each of you will bring your hands in front of you, displaying a certain number of fingers. The number you choose to display is up to you. You might choose to hold out three fingers or nine fingers. With each of you showing your fingers, your challenge is to add up the total on both your hands and your partner's hands and then be the first to yell out that total. If your partner shows four fingers and you show three, then the person to yell 'seven' first is the winner. Any questions? Great, let's play! 1, 2, 3, go!" (Play three or four rounds.)

"Person A now reflects on the activity, asking as many different 'Did you notice …?' questions as possible (allow 3 minutes).

QUESTIONS
- What were some of the most interesting, "Did you notice …?" questions?
- What made those particularly interesting to you?

Lecture: Noticing • • • • • • • • • • • • • • • • • •

(For more on observation, see Chapter 3)

MAIN POINTS
- What you notice dramatically impacts the quality of the reflective process.
- Some things are better to notice than others.

SAY THIS

"Did you notice that the way you phrase the first question sets the tone and direction for the reflection process? That ought to indicate to us that what we notice is critical. Notice what you are noticing right now. Many of you are focused on me, but some might still be thinking about the activity or the discussion. Others are noticing different aspects of the room or maybe a nagging headache or other body pain. You may even notice as I ran through that list, your attention shifted through the different things I was calling out, finally resting on that nagging pain in your body! Our attention is critical. Every moment of our life we are processing a huge amount of stimulation. Most of it is unremarkable and gets little attention.

"When you watch a group in a structured experience, where does your attention go? What kinds of things do you notice? Here are a couple of reliable places to start each time you are facilitating a group.

"Leadership: Who took leadership? Did the group accept them? Why? Were they effective?

"Conflict: How did the group get along? What kinds of conflict were present? Was there a conflict between what the group wanted to achieve and what they actually achieved?

"Communication: How well did the group communicate? Was everyone's opinion respected? Who tended to make the decisions? Was anyone left out? Why?"

Activity: Push Pull
PROCEDURE

"For this next activity, B will observe and process while A and C play. This activity is called Push Pull. A and C need to stand on one foot and grab hands in a fireman's grip, with each holding the other's wrist. The objective is to strategically try to push or pull your opponent off balance. Ready, go!"

After A and C have played, B leads the reflective discussion.

Lecture: Genuine Curiosity
MAIN POINT

• Cultivating a spirit of curiosity brings more meaning to your reflection.

SAY THIS

"What were you curious about as you were asking questions? Did you already believe you knew the answers? When facilitating an activity, see what happens if you adopt a position of genuine curiosity, asking questions you are genuinely curious about. Connect with the spirit of your internal five-year-old—that little kid inside of you who has endless curiosity. As you reflect and ask questions, notice if you are really curious or just walking through the motions. Think through The 5 Questions in your mind. Ask questions in such a way that you become truly curious at every turn."

Activity: Gotcha

PROCEDURE

"For our final triad activity, A and B will play while C gets a chance to process. A and B face each other and take your right hands and place them palm up toward your partner. Now take your left index fingers and point them down directly in the center of your partner's palm. On the count of three, you will try to grab your partner's index finger and at the same time try to keep your index finger from being captured. 1, 2, 3, go!"

Person C now processes that experience.

Activity: Count Off

PROCEDURE

"Now that each of you has had an opportunity to lead the reflective discussion following an experience, the challenge is to facilitate a group through an experience.

"I need each of the teams of three to join with two other groups to make groups of nine people each. In each group, designate a facilitator who will observe and process the entire group through this last experience.

"For the group, your challenge is to count from one to twenty. Simple enough. There are, however, some rules:

1.   Everyone must say at least one number.

2.   The group may not use an organized pattern, for instance just going around the circle. The numbers must be random.

3.   No one may indicate to any person when they should or should not say a number. No subtle coughs or pointing to help out. Each person must decide when s/he will say a number.

4.   No two people can say the same number at the same time. If this happens, the entire group must start over from one.

"Ready. Begin." (Groups play for 5 to 7 minutes.)

"Facilitators, it is now your opportunity to provide closure for your group on that experience. Start with 'Did you notice ...?' and move smoothly through The 5 Questions. Go!"

After the groups have had a chance to facilitate, lead a brief closure of the workshop. Have participants celebrate the questions their facilitator asked. Encourage them to explore the power of The 5 Questions and how they might apply to the context of the group (in the classroom, on the challenge course, in professional development, etc.)

Acknowledgements

This book could not have been written without the dedication, thought, and brilliance of our colleague and friend, Mary Beth Campbell. Mary Beth served with us at every stage of the creation of this book, from development of the concept through initial draft editing. We are deeply indebted. Carolyn Hill also helped tremendously with these ideas and has presented them with incredible effectiveness for several years. Carolyn specifically introduced the changes we have made to questions 4 and 5 in the model and taught us how these changes produced better outcomes for groups.

Many of the concepts for this book were created through our mutual contact with and work for the Link Crew and WEB programs. Phil Boyte created both programs and has served as a mentor and adviser to us for years. We are thankful for the opportunities, guidance, and friendship he always provided.

We received tremendous support from the thousands of Link Crew and WEB teachers who have been through our trainings. They are the champions working to make schools better places for kids.

A book is just a dream until it is written and published. And this book might well have stayed a dream if not for Mony Cunningham and Dave Wood of Wood N Barnes Publishing. We are thankful for their patience, persistence, and belief in our ability to write our ideas.

Finally, Jeanie, Moe, Tenaya and Aidan Jacobson; Marty Ruddy, Chris Klebl, and Kylea Taylor have all our love. We would not be who we are without their love and support.

References

BOOKS

Bloom, B., Englehart, M., Furst, E., Hill, W. & Krathwohl, D. (1956). *Taxonomy of educational objectives: The classification of educational goals. Handbook I: Cognitive domain.* New York, Toronto: Longmans, Green.

Bohm, D. (1996). *On dialogue.* New York: Routledge.

Brookfield, S. D. (1986). *Understanding and facilitating adult learning.* San Francisco: Jossey-Bass.

Cozolino, L. (2002). *The neuroscience of psychotherapy.* New York: Norton and Company.

Dewey, J. (1938). *Experience and education.* New York: Touchstone.

Dilts, R. (2003). *From coach to awakener.* Cupertino, CA: Meta Publications.

Dweck, C. S. (2006). *Mindset.* New York: Ballantine Books.

Fluegelman, Andrew, ed. (1981). *More new games.* Garden City, NY: Dolphin Books/Doubleday & Company, Inc.

Garmston, R. & Wellman, B. (1997). *The adaptive school, developing and facilitating collaborative groups.* El Dorado Hill, CA: Four Hats Press.

Isaacs, W. (1999). *Dialogue and the art of thinking together.* New York: Doubleday.

Jensen, E. (2008). *Brain based learning.* Thousand Oaks, CA: Corwin Press.

Jensen, F. E. with Nutt, A. E. (2015). *The teenage brain.* New York: Harper Collins.

Kaner, S. (1996). *Facilitator's guide to participatory decision-making.* Gabriola Island, BC, Canada: New Society Publishers.

Kolb, D. A. (1984). *Experiential learning.* Englewood Cliffs, NJ: Prentice Hall.

Kotulak, R. (1996). *Inside the brain.* Kansas City, MO: Andrew McMeel Publishing.

Levine, M. (2002). *A mind at a time.* New York: Simon & Schuster.

Lewin,K. (1947). Frontiers of group dynamics: Concept, method and reality in social science, social equilibria, and social change. *Human Relations, 1,*5-41.

Luria, A. R. (1973). *The working brain.* New York: Basic Books.

Medina, J. (2008). *Brain rules.* Seattle, WA: Pear Press.

Neisser, B., & Saran, R. (2004). *Enquiring minds: Socratic dialogue in education.* Stoke on Trent, ST4 5NP, United Kingdom, Trentham Books Limited.

Pfeiffer, W. & Jones, J. E. (1975). *A handbook of structured experiences for human relations training.* La Jolla, CA: University Associates.

Piaget, J. (1976). *Peaget Sampler: An introduction to Jean Piaget through his own words.* NY: Wiley.

Rohnke, K. (1984). *Silver bullets: A guide to initiative problems, adventure, games and trust activities.* Dubuque, IA: Kendall Hunt Publishing.

Sousa, D. A. (2010). *Mind, brain, and education: Neuroscience implications for the classroom.* Bloomington, IN: Solution Tree Press.

Stanchfield, J. (2014). *Inspired educator, inspired learner.* Bethany, OK: Wood N Barnes Publishing.

Thompson, J. (2004). *CASC staff development leadership handbook.* CASC.

Williamson, M. (1996). *A return to love: Reflections on the principles of "A course in miracles."* San Francisco: HarperOne.

Web Sites

Experiential Learning Cycles, James Neill. http://www.wilderdom.com/experiential/, July 5, 2015

Experiential Learning Articles and Critiques of David Kolb's Theory, Tim Pickles. http://reviewing.co.uk/research/experiential.learning.htm, June 30, 2015

What is Experiential Learning? www.teamskillstraining.co.uk/tst_article1.htm, June 30, 2015.

Learning Theories and Transfer of Learning. www.otec.uoregon.edu/learning_theory.htm, July 5, 2015

Learning from Experience. www.learningfromexperience.com Hit the Research Library, this takes you to several Kolb articles and the link to a 160-page bibliography on experiential learning theory.

Additional Resources

There are DOZENS of online resources for games, activities, demonstrations, and activities. Here are a few that are useful and active as of July, 2015:

GAMES

GAMES

http://www.businessballs.com/teambuilding.htm
http://www.experientialtools.com/
http://www.wilderdom.com/games/
http://www.fundoing.com/resources.html
http://www.ultimatecampresource.com/site/camp-activities/ice-breakers.html
http://www.funandgames.org/games/GameHomePage.htm

SIMULATIONS

http://tenntlc.utk.edu/simulations-and-gaming-for-experiential-learning/
http://www.creativeteachingsite.com/edusims.html
http://theconnectedclassroom.wikispaces.com/Simulations
http://www.edutopia.org/online-simulations-classroom

BOOKS

Again, there are many books on this topic ... our favorites include

Campbell, M. B., Hill, C. Jacobson, M. *Springboard* (2009)

Cavert, C. *Portable Teambuilding Activities* (2015), *Games for Groups* (1999), *Games for Teachers* w/L. Frank (2000), Affordable Portables (1999)

Frank, Laurie. *Journey Toward the Caring Classroom, 2nd Edition* (2013), *Leading Together* (2008)

Rohnke, K. *Funn N' Games* (2004), *Silver Bullets* (1984), *Quicksilver* (1995), *Cowstails and Cobras* (1997)

Stanchfield, J. *Inspired educator, inspired learner.* (2014), *Tips & Tools,* (2007)

About the Authors

Micah Jacobson has presented to over 1,000,000 students, educators, and parents throughout North America since 1990. He has been a trainer for the United Nation Youth Forum, The Association of Young Leaders in Russia, student leadership organizations throughout the US and Canada including NASC, FBLA, CSLC and many others. The core of Micah's work has always been experiential education.

As a cofounder of The Boomerang Project, Micah co-leads its nationally recognized transition and orientation programs, Link Crew and WEB. Link Crew and WEB together reach more than 4 million freshmen and 6th graders each fall in more than 4,000 schools in 6 different countries, helping to create positive school climates where kids feel comfortable, engaged, and successful. The Boomerang Project also produces outstanding faculty in-service, teacher training, and Open to Outcome Workshops.

Micah holds an MBA from the University of Michigan and in addition to working in education has been a manager for both consulting and technology companies. His passion continues to be working to help people engage more actively in their own lives.

Mari Ruddy is a speaker, writer and educator. She's been a high school Spanish teacher, Activities Director, and a school Assistant Principal and Principal. In addition, she helped start over 35 Big Picture Learning high schools throughout the United States.

Mari owned a small company that trained people with diabetes to be endurance athletes. Mari got involved as an American Diabetes Association volunteer and she created Team Red and the Red Rider Program for cyclists with diabetes, which are used at the more than 85 Tour de Cure rides across the United States. There are now more than 10,000 cyclists with diabetes who wear the Red Rider jersey Mari created.

Mari earned an MA in Educational Leadership from San Jose State University. She lives and exercises in Minneapolis, Minnesota. You can learn more about Mari at her website: www.mariruddy.com.

Open to Outcome Workshops/Programs

Open to Outcome workshops are powerful learning experiences that give teachers, facilitators, camp directors and outdoor educators all the tools they need to lead and reflect on experiential activities. Getting people actively engaged in learning opens the door to incredible, life changing moments. Facilitators are trained to gently guide participants toward internal reflection by using an open ended questioning model that helps them discover the learning that is true for them.

In the Open to Outcome workshop, we go beyond the text to engage facilitators and educators in a step-by-step guide to not only processing an experience, but also presenting and developing powerful material.

In the two-day course of you will master:
- Designing Experiential Curriculum and Workshops
- Setting Up Powerful Learning Experiences
- More than 15 Hands-on Activities
- The 5 Questions Model of Debriefing
- Learning Cycle and Group Development Theory

Open to Outcome is also available as a powerful faculty in-service program. Programs can be designed to fit partial or whole day agendas.

For more information about booking an Open to Outcome workshop, please contact:

The Boomerang Project
PO Box 600
Santa Cruz, CA 95061
831-460-7040 • 800-688-7578
www.boomerangproject.com

Micah Jacobson
micah@boomerangproject.com

Mari Ruddy
mari@mariruddy.com